Shop Graphics

Shop Graphics

Shop Graphics

Published and distributed in Europe and Latin America by:
Index Book, S.L.
Consell de Cent, 160, local 3
08015 Barcelona
Tel.: +34 93 454 55 47   Fax: +34 93 454 84 38
E-mail: ib@indexbook.com
www.indexbook.com

Copyright © 2009 by **maomao** publications
Publisher: Paco Asensio
Editorial coordination: Anja Llorella Oriol
Editor and texts: Claire Dalquié
Copy-editing: Benjamin Brinner
Art Director: Emma Termes Parera
Layout: Maira Purman
Cover design: Emma Termes Parera
Cover image: Blok Design para Caban

ISBN-13: 978-84-92643-20-2

Printed in Spain

All rights reserved. No part of this publication
may be reproduced or transmitted in any form or
by any means, electronic or mechanical, including
photocopy, recording or any information storage
and retrieval system, without permission in writing
from the copyright owner(s).

The captions and artwork in this book are based
on material supplied by the designers whose work
is included. While every effort has been made to
ensure their accuracy, maomao does under any
circumstances accept any responsibility for any
error or omissions.

Introduction 9

Ladies First 13
Sita Murt 14
Inversa 20
Ross + Bute 24
Van-Dos 28
Rodebjer 34
Lemon Chic 38
NOJESS 44

Grooms & Blooms 49
Gibson 50
Paraiso 56
Duchamp 60
Institut Parfumeur Flores 64
Zekka 70
Hayford & Rhodes 76

His 'n' Hers 81
Actually... 82
Greta & Luis 90
Levi's 94
Lovem 102
PARISTEXAS 106
Wooonderland 114

Snack Attack 121
Afro Coffee 122
Natcha 126
Unpackaged 132
Cacao Sampaka 136
The Larder 144

Pamper, Adorn and Indulge 149
Korres 150
Tatty Devine 158
Lascivious 164
Content 168
Women´Secret 176
Fabrications 182
Bla Bla Bra 186
Tabooboo 194
Prosays' 200

Supersizing 207
PUB 208
Parad 216
Caban 222
Fena 226
Naked 234
Inspiration 240
Marui 244

Creed & Concepts 253
Bozar Shop 254
Chapter 2 258
Dissidence by Boris 264
Hitherto 268
Test Tube 276
Pierpoint 280
Skanno 284
Wawas Barcelona Shop 290

Elusive Exclusives 295
Preen 296
Mahna Mahna 306
Expo Nova 310
Hayashi 316
Melynas 322
Pedro García 326

Introduction

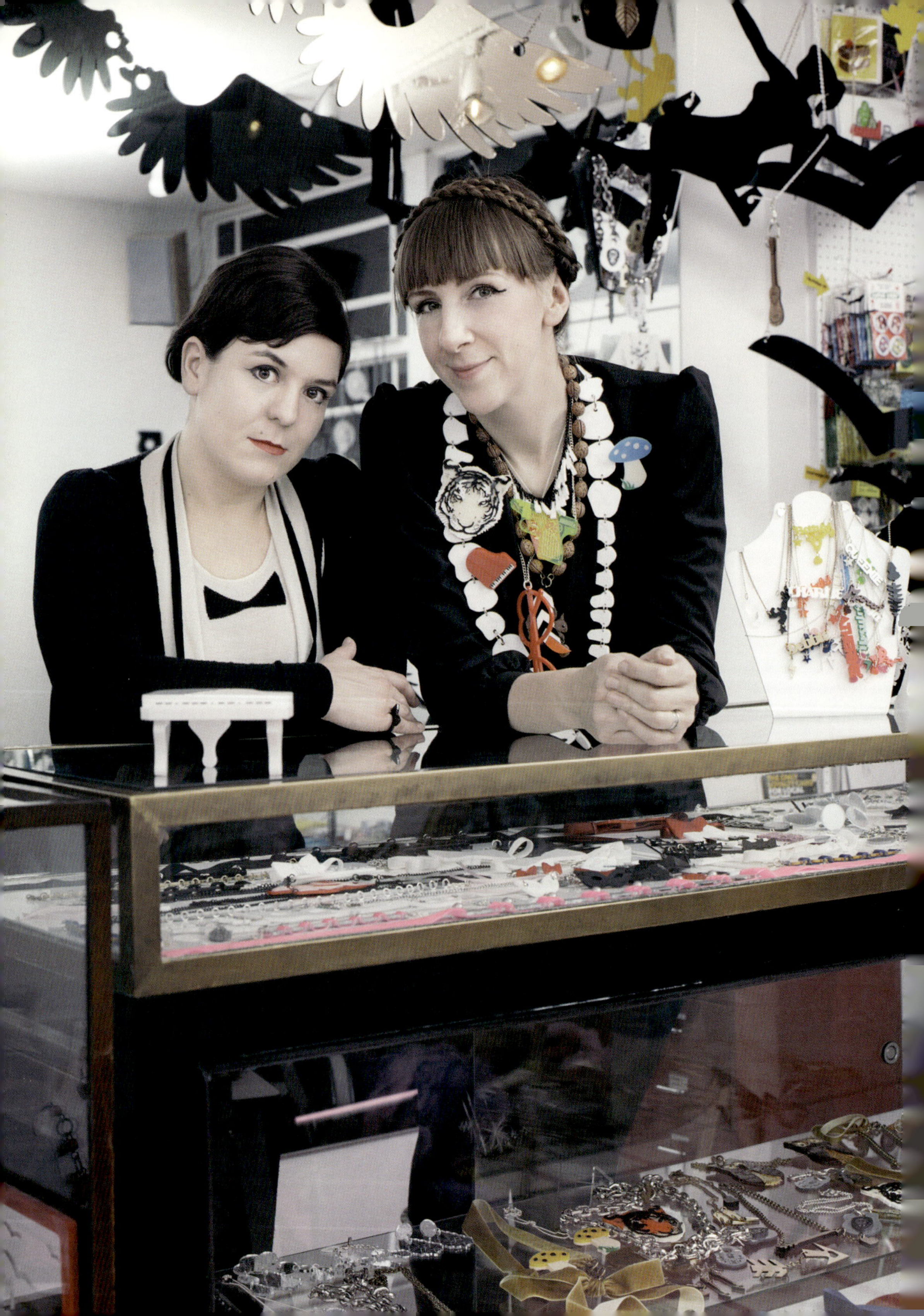

Brands these days are like bundles of reference and connotation. Not only do they suggest the consumer's visual and aesthetic preferences, they just might bare your soul: social background, taste in music, purchasing power... are you a sports freak or technology geek? Recycle much? Just how terrible is your sense of humor? Some brand identities even have a political agenda and aren't shy about it. Why should they be, if their customers aren't?

The word "identity" has two meanings: one applies to the special characteristics that make something individual and distinctive, while the other describes the quality of being identical. These are radical opposites, and the meaning we are interested in as far as defining a brand's visual statement would obviously be the first one – it is needless to say that every company aims to be unique. However, the current market does somehow nurture competitive difference within a web of similarity. The connection between difference and similarity is very peculiar in our mental idea of originality, because we desire the original, desired by others, not just because we find pleasure in difference, but because we wish to be desired also. In the end, if it is to present a coordinated look and leave a memorable and lasting impression, a brand identity will most probably have a corporate logo, a chosen typeface and a chromatic palette. Sameness and difference are both inevitable, so why not explore both of them with open minds?

Many brands that stand out in today's fashion and product market embrace this idea. On one hand, a classic corporate identity with logo, typeface, corporate colors, etc, focused and consistent throughout, and on the other hand, a one-of-a-kind esoteric marketing weapon – the brand statement! A concise brand statement will ensure that a brand has continuity, and continuity is a key element in establishing a marketing identity. A brand statement might have come about after tireless research on consumer and drive sales, or from the need to express one's personality, it could have come from wanting to identify with a specific community or derived from simply aspiring to convey a sense of purpose. The concept behind London's Unpackaged store identity comes from a real set of values which the owners ruthlessly apply to its entirety – everything in the store, from interior and products to marketing and services, is organic, sustainable and environmentally-friendly. The Inspiration store in Sweden wants to provide an array of inexpensive and useful items – the ideal place to browse around for one of those great utilitarian Scandinavian design gifts. On the other end of the spectrum, but no less important, Wooonderland in Singapore wants shopping to be an overall fun experience akin to a class of six-year-olds inside a candy shop, and Lemon Chic in Mexico is the answer from heaven for those who strive to remain fashionably au courant no matter what, thanks to a personalized shopping program.

Whatever the selling proposition may be, it requires a dedicated push from the graphic designer to make an identity click (with the brand), tune in (with the clients) and stand out (from the crowd). Rather than obsessing about their competitors or trying to overshadow others, the selection of brands, graphic designers and design studios in this book have sought after their own direction, benefited from inspiration and added a special dimension to their work. Put down those shopping bags, take a seat and have a look.

Ladies First

What we have here are brands that cater to a cross-cultural, international brigade of economically powerful women looking for products and services that meet their criteria: identities that are feminine and sophisticated, occasionally indulging in girly frills for the younger set, but without losing a casual edge that epitomizes a relaxed elegance. Simple chromatic palettes give an overall sense of blissful simplicity, while small details and finishing touches adorning the tags, carrier bags and brochures are sure to appeal to true fashionistas.

Sita Murt

Cla-se, www.cla-se.com

As one of Spain's leading designers in women's fashion, one of the core attributes of Sita Murt's coveted collections is knits, a technique she famously loves to investigate and experiment with. Design studio Cla-se designed a simple "mix and match" corporate identity and matching banners, on which a scratchy ink pen doodle, reminiscent of a textile weave, is the running thread.

Avinyó, 18
08002 Barcelona
Spain
www.sitamurt.com

Sita Murt believes in sensations and searches for the softest yarns for her creations.

15

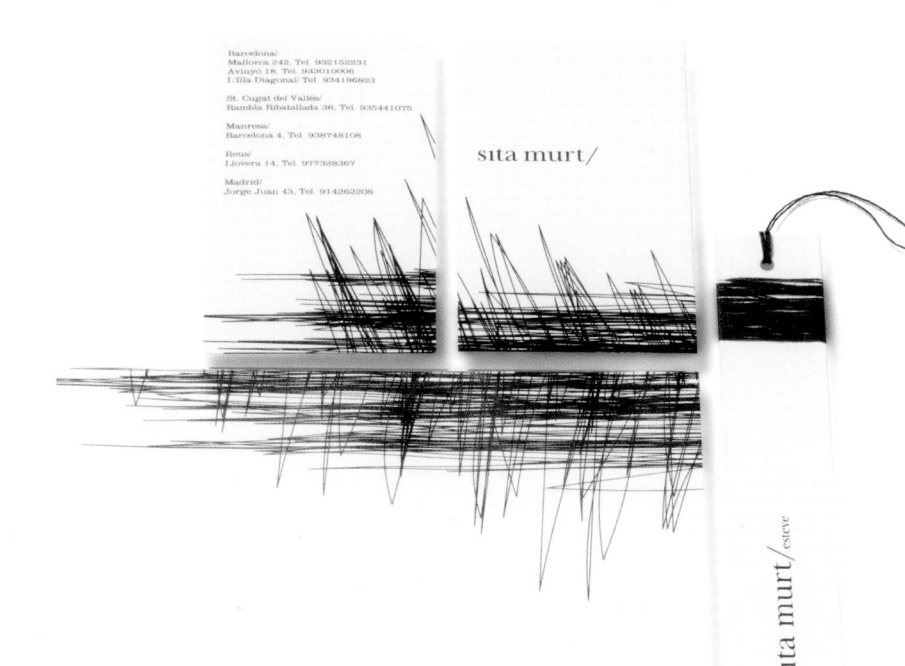

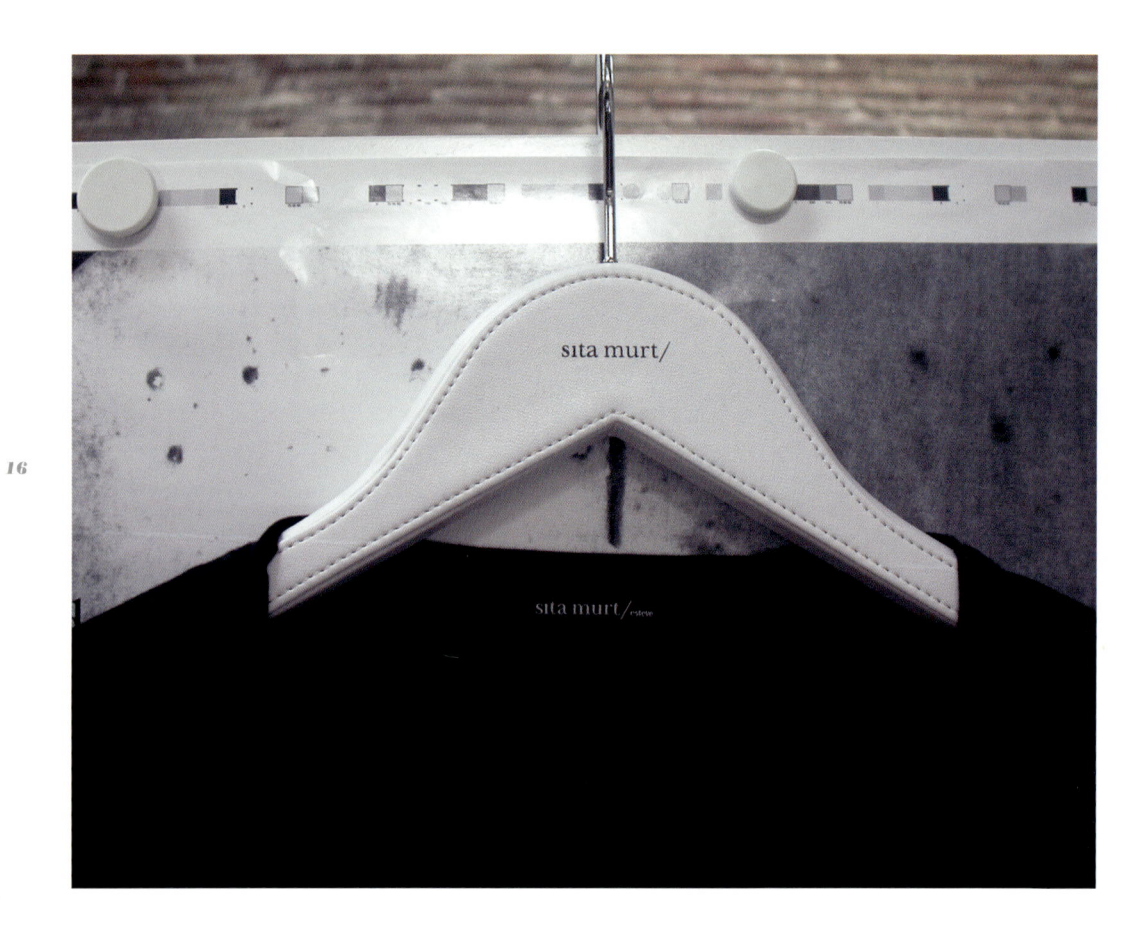

The simple and subtle brand logo can be applied repeatedly in the store without being overwhelming.

17

Banners featuring the "scribble" graphic outside the stores and woven cotton garment tags.

sita murt/esteve
sita murt/esteve
sita murt/esteve

sita murt/esteve
sita murt/esteve

Inversa

Sala 2, www.sala-2.com.ar

With a fresh new style and direction every season, Sala 2's branding for Inversa, a label for young women aged between 15 and 30, mutates as often as its target demographic. Each season's theme dictates the collection's aesthetic, along with the look of the website, window displays, print and promotional materials, paying special attention to the fun die-cut swing tags.

Av. Santa Fe 1987
Buenos Aires,
1123 Capital Federal
Argentine Republic
www.inversanet.com.ar

The store's decoration and color combos also change to match each new collection.

21

VADAVIA 112 L.11 (QUILMES)
22 (BERAZATEGUI)
ESTER) 48 N°611 (LA PLATA)
DELA 337 **(OUTLET)** QUILMES

WWW.INVERSANET.COM.AR

Sweets a go-go announce the coming of spring, while plaid and tailoring tips warn of colder weather.

Ross + Bute

Form, www.form.uk.com

Clothing label Anonymous has a new name: Ross + Bute. London studio Form was given the task of designing their new logo, which incorporates both the new and the former names so as not to disorient clients. It creates a recognizable identity which represents the label's feminine clothing, as well as being easy to incorporate into their stationery and new flagship shop in Notting Hill.

57 Ledbury Road
Notting Hill
London W11 2AA
United Kingdom
www.anonymousclothing.com

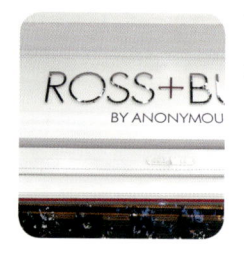

The metallic outdoor signage highlights the logo, translated as silver foil block on cards and tags.

ROSS+BUTE
BY ANONYMOUS

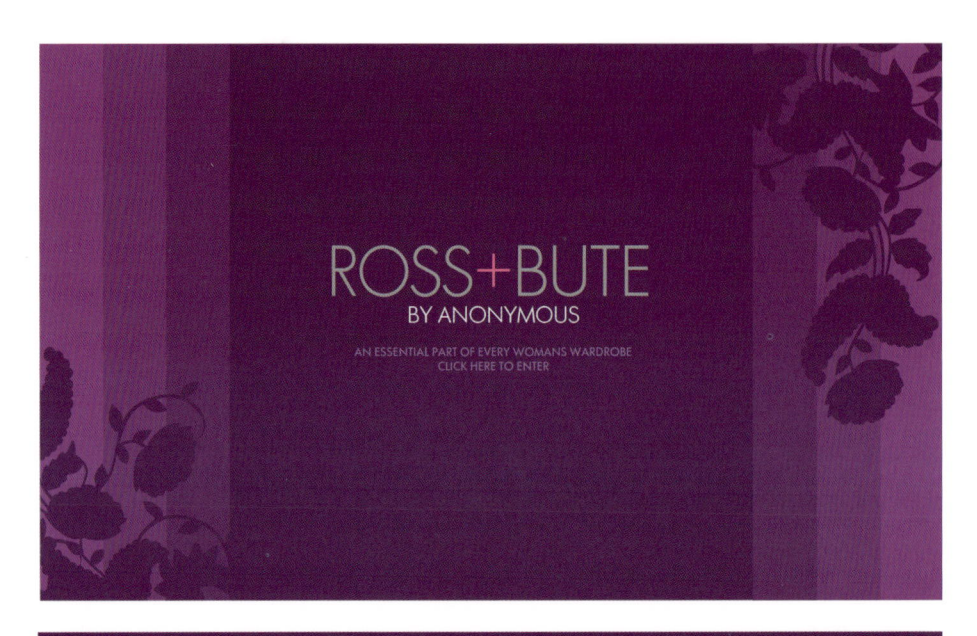

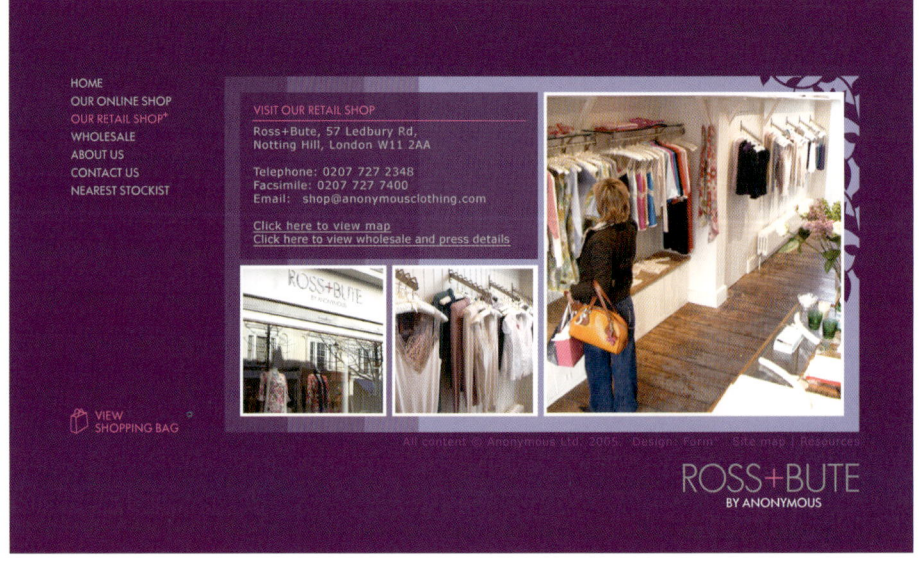

A deep plum color unifies all the corporate identity pieces, from carrier bags to the website.

Lindy Ross, Director
Mobile: 07973 848 747
Email: lindy@anonymousclothing.com

Head Office: Anonymous Limited
19 Baseline Studios, Whitchurch Road, London W11 4AT
Telephone: 020 7727 2370 Fax: 020 7168 2465
Email: info@anonymousclothing.com

Shop: Ross+Bute by Anonymous
57 Ledbury Road, N...
Telephone: 020 772...
Email: shop@anonymous...
www.anonymous...

Van-Dos

Andrew McConochie Design & Communication, www.andrewmcconochie.com

Based in Madrid and Tokyo, Andrew McConochie Design & Communication is an independent design studio that focuses on the fashion, beauty and art industries. Their logo and branding for Spanish fashion brand Van-Dos was carefully chosen to reflect the brand's style and chromatic palette, which is neutral and discreet, so as to bring the elaborate patterns of the clothes to the forefront.

Available at La Provenza
Goya, 68
28001 Madrid
Spain
www.van-dos.com

Van-Dos's versatile pieces blend good design and comfort, a prerequisite for 21st-century life.

29

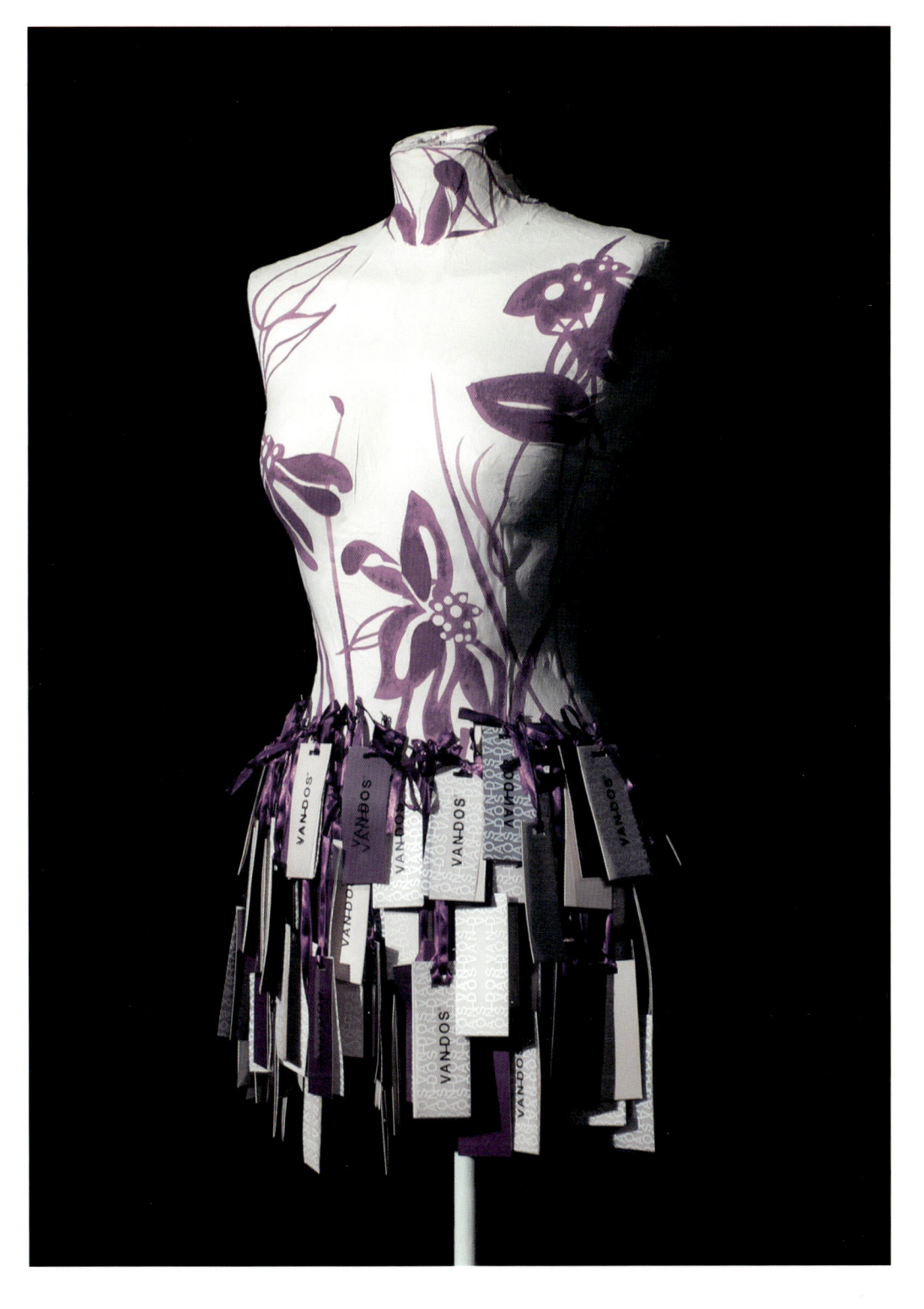

The use of transparencies and textures adds a distinguished touch to the corporate identity.

30

31

The catalog's design reflects the uncluttered, romantic and feminine feel of the clothes.

33

Rodebjer

Stefania Malmsten, www.stefania.se

A brand known for strong its fresh approach to fashion, Rodebjer combines casual and classical elegance with a youthful sensibility. The concept for the first store was developed by Stefania Malmsten: a strong identity program based on black and white, and a unique modular shop interior where boxes are made to accommodate not only clothes, but also things that have inspired the collections.

Jakobsbergsgatan 6
111 44 Stockholm
Sweden
www.rodebjer.com

Window displays are designed by illustrator/set designer Liselotte Watkins and changed regularly.

Store
Jakobsbergsgatan 6
111 44 Stockholm, Sweden
phone +46 8 410 450 95
store@rodebjer.com
www.rodebjer.com

RODEBJER

The clothes are wrapped in cellophane bags with the logo and a seasonal card (here, Spring/Summer 08).

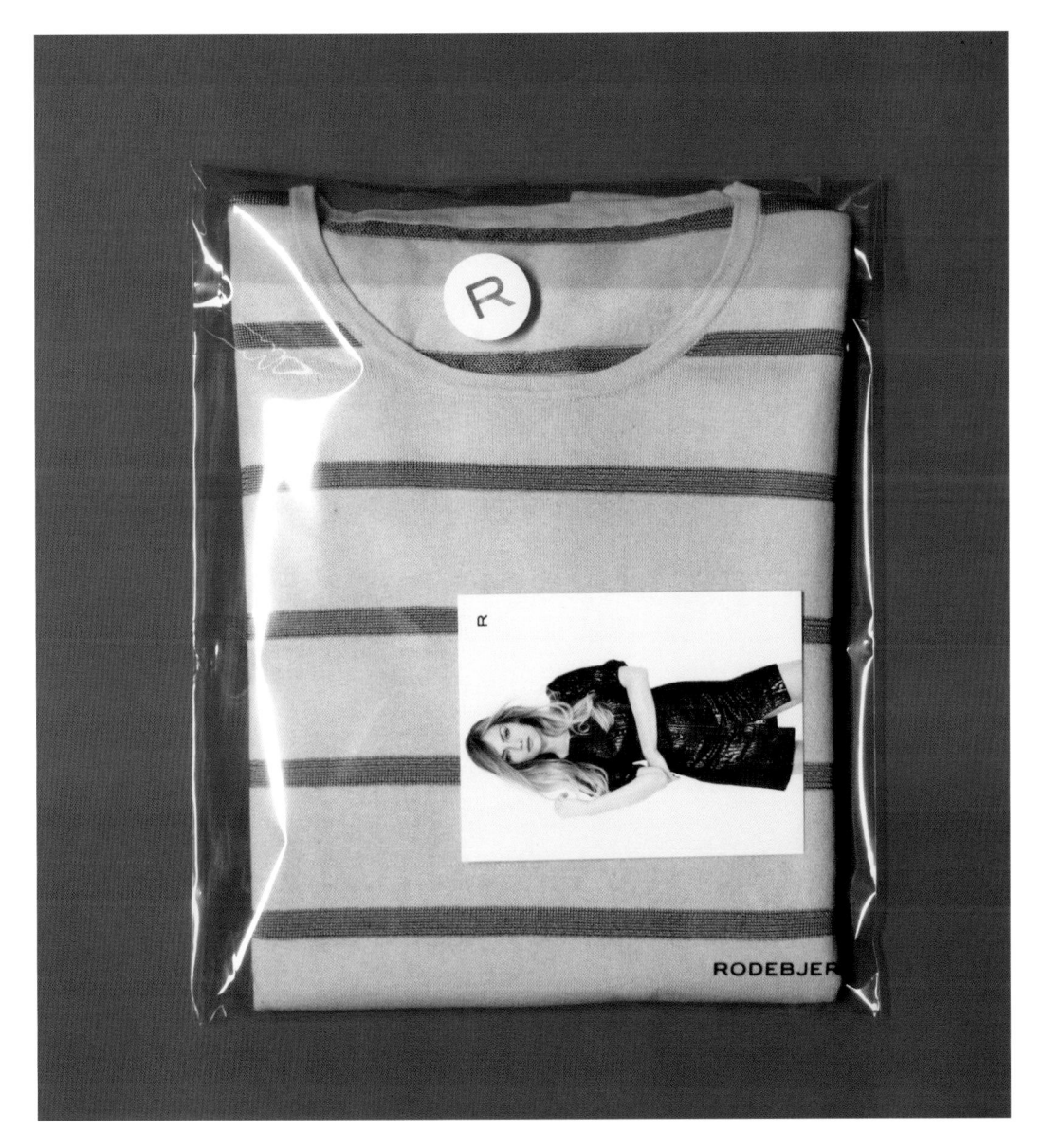

Lemon Chic

La Tortilleria, www.latortilleria.com

A boutique for customers that want to be dressed with the latest trends from head to toe, Lemon Chic delivers cosmopolitan fashion. Mexican studio La Tortilleria's delectable visual identity for the store mixes floral imagery with a dot-matrix logo, suggesting feminine and modern women, while shades of cream, canary yellow and lime green suggest the sweet and sour delights of a lemon meringue pie.

Calzada del Valle No. 201
Planta Alta
San Pedro, 66220
Mexico
www.lemonchic.com

Lemon Chic runs an Image Consultant Program that assists clients in building up their wardrobe.

LEMON CHIC
SWEET AND SOUR GLAM

REBECCA TAYLOR . CATHERINE MALANDRINO . CHLOÉ . BARTAK
TRACEY REESE . MIGUELINA . YANUK . BALENCIAGA . FRANKIE
ADRIANO GOLDSCHMIED . EARNST SEWN . JOYSTICK . BLUE CU
JOE'S . ROCK AND REPUBLIC . GERARD YOSCA . NANETTE LEP

10

Simplified versions of the floral imagery creep plant-like across the store's walls and print matter.

LEMON CHIC

fall winter 2006

LEMON CHIC
SWEET AND SOUR GLAM

skulls
A Fashion Statement

ALEXANDER McQUEEN
RICH & SKINNY JEANS
TYLIE MALIBU

LEMON CHIC

Print adverts and newsletters feature a seasonal theme and inform of the latest brand arrivals.

NOJESS

Bob Foundation, www.bobfoundation.com

Art directors and designers Mitsunori Asakura and Hiromi Suzuki, known for their delicious work in print and paper, created a Christmas promotion for Japanese fashion brand NOJESS with the theme of "Eternity Blinking." Conjuring images of icy landscapes, the Northern sky and constellations, their graphics spread across tags, brochures and carrier bags, as well as in theatrical Christmas displays.

20-11 Daikanyama-cho
Shibuya-ku
Tokyo 150-0034
Japan
www.nojess.net

Girlishness, femininity and accessories are key at NOJESS – their presentation is always exquisite.

45

46

The visual theme is adapted to all items through a collage of photograph, drawings and embroideries.

47

Grooms
& Blooms

Whether he is tinged with a retro flavor or defiantly postmodern, the Perfect Gentleman will never go out of style. The good old days of dressing to the nines and bringing flowers to your sweetheart are modernized by adding a contemporary touch to vintage ideals, revisiting today's classics with a nostalgic twist. The explosive opposing effects of old and new, contrasting materials or careless chic strike again, as demonstrated here by a selection of international florists and suit-makers for the modern dandy.

Gibson

The Coöp, www.theco-op.net.au

New Zealand menswear label Gibson approached Coöp to develop an identity concept to target the youthful inner-city corporate man. The branding was inspired by early 20th-century social observer Charles Dana Gibson and reinterpreted into modern themes of voyeurism and the ideal self. A patterning system, typographic system and a series of illustrations were developed for a variety of brand applications.

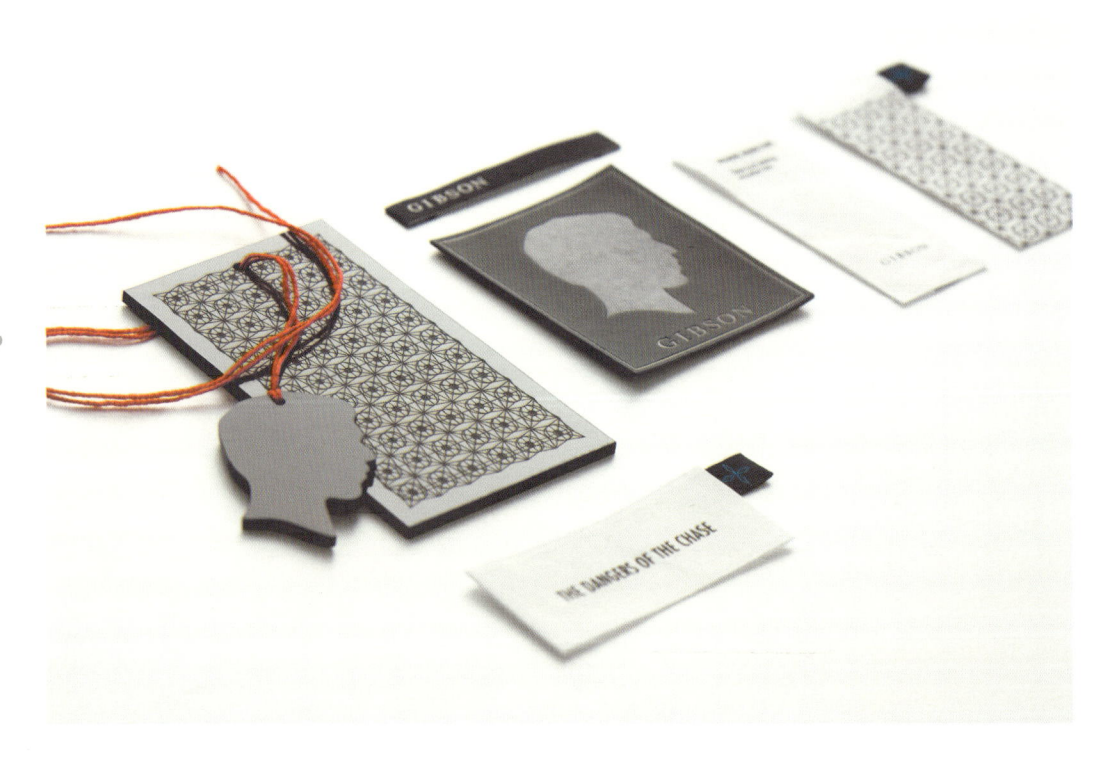

436 George Street
Sydney, NSW 2000
Australia
www.gibsonclothing.com.au

Captions from Charles Dana Gibson's illustrations are used on swing tickets and retail displays.

Morning suit for gentlemen of means.

Show them you mean business with this *medium weight black pin stripe suit* that boasts a modern contrasting inner lining.

Morning suit for gentlemen of means.

the turning of the

Tide

51

52

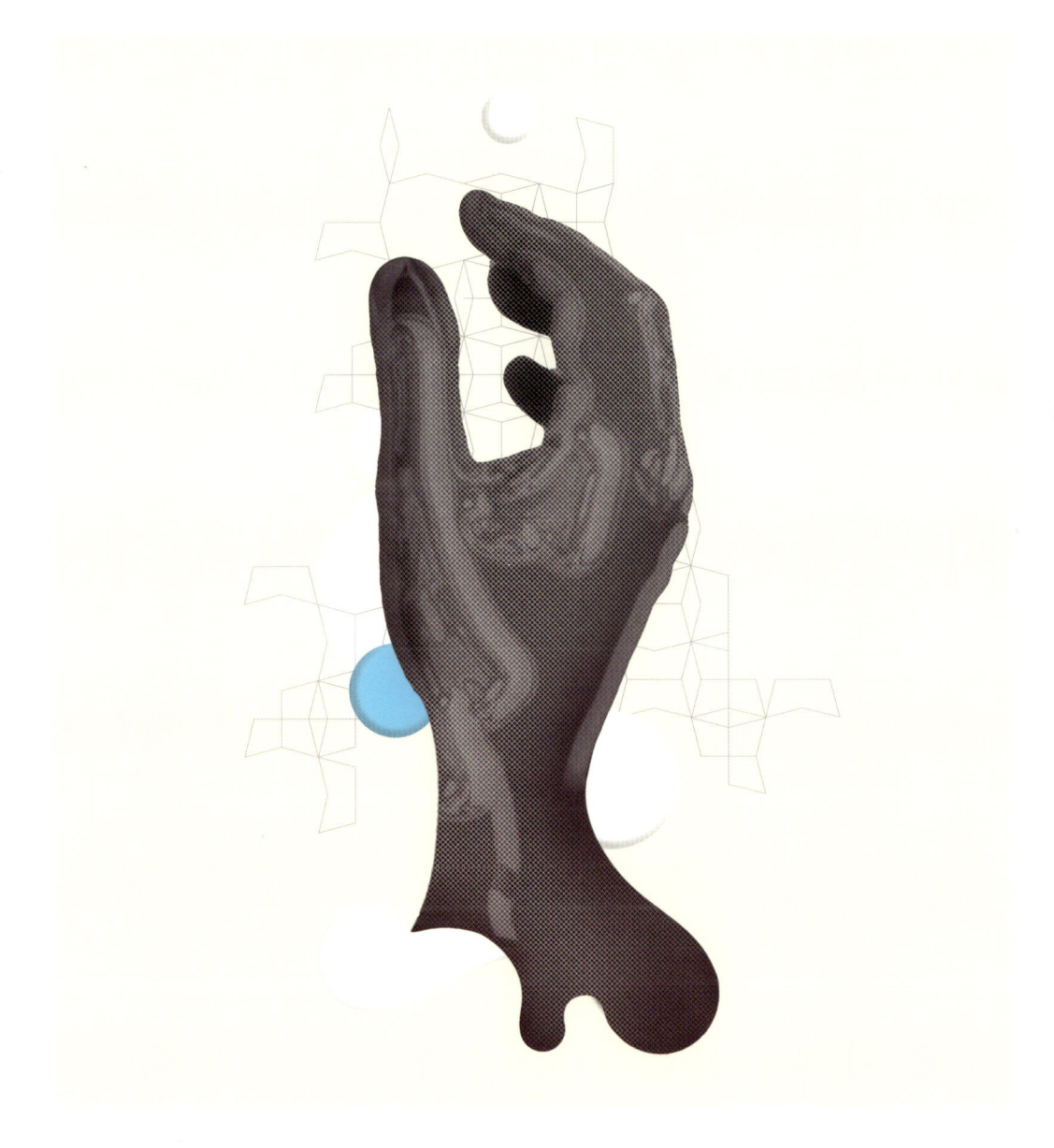

The use of reflective materials and anatomic illustrations reinforce the theme of the ideal self.

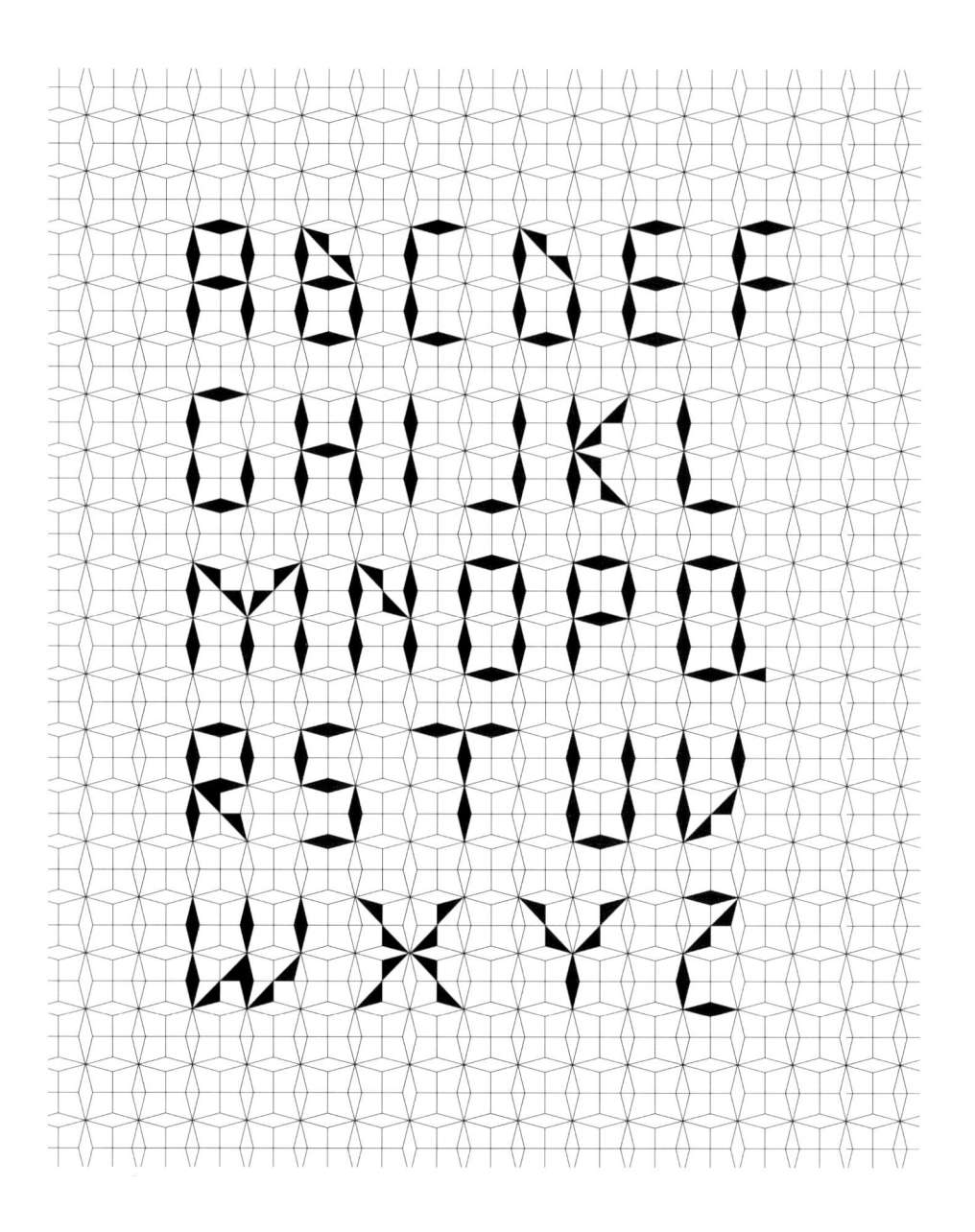

Period illustration inspired a modern patterning system used as a grid for a secondary brand typeface.

GIBSON

Paraíso

Sala 2, www.sala-2.com.ar

A flower shop with a strong sense of aesthetics, the concept of contrast is prevalent throughout the flower arrangements, bouquets and the store interior of Paraíso, decorated with second-hand classical objects in combination with very modern building materials. Sala 2's packaging for the store mixes silk paper and silk-screened glass paper, adorned with a classic large-sized note card.

Juramento 3311
Buenos Aires,
1430 Capital Federal
Argentine Republic
www.floresparaiso.com.ar

Paraíso uses atypical flower species to create unusual combinations of colors and aromas.

57

High-contrast identity and wall graphics follow the store's "marriage of opposites" concept.

59

Duchamp

FOUR IV, www.fouriv.com

Having established itself as the ultimate men's accessories brand, Duchamp enlisted FOUR IV to help re-launch the brand with a new suite of packaging items to reflect the new brand image: matte-black materials with glossy black foils set off the rich colors and strong patterns that are the brand's signature and neatly echo the store interior's use of black glass, leather panels and Dada-inspired iconography.

155 Regent Street
London W1B 4JE
United Kingdom
www.duchamplondon.com

The materials chosen for the store interior reflect a "contemporary men's dressing room" feel.

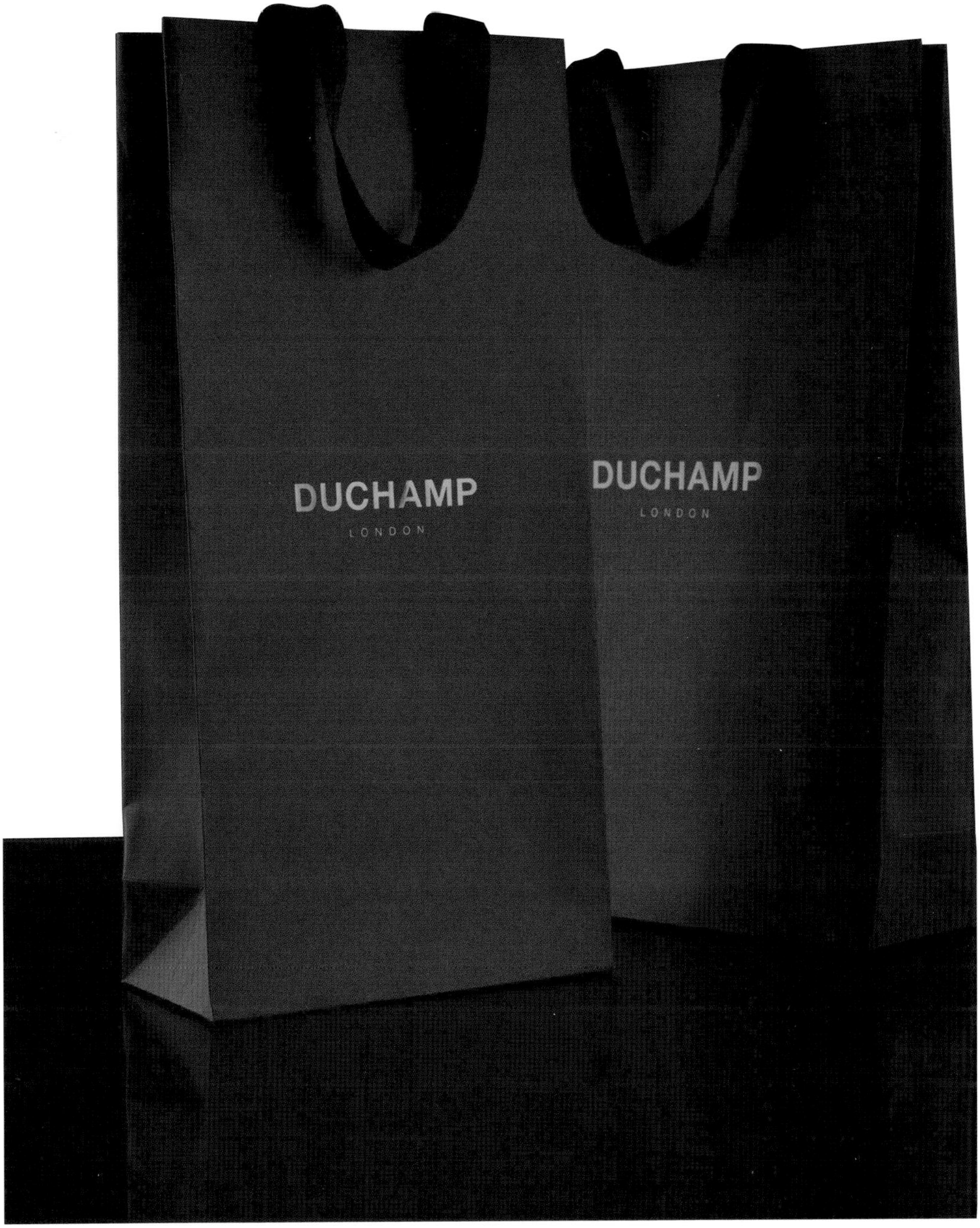
DUCHAMP
LONDON
DUCHAMP
LONDON

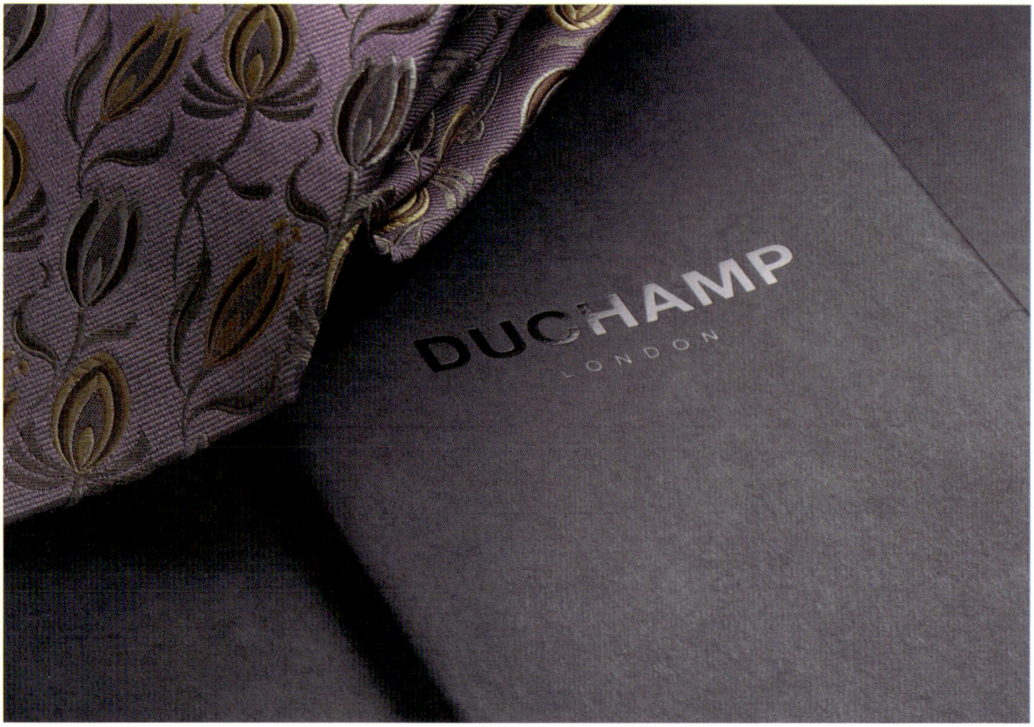
DUCHAMP
LONDON

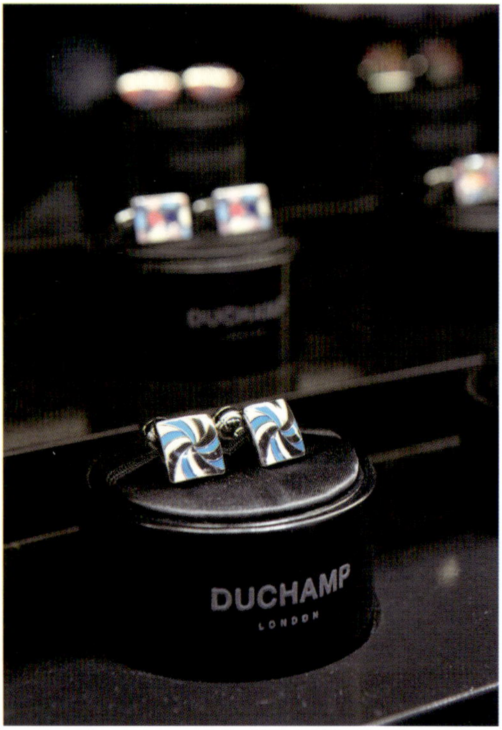
DUCHAMP
LONDON

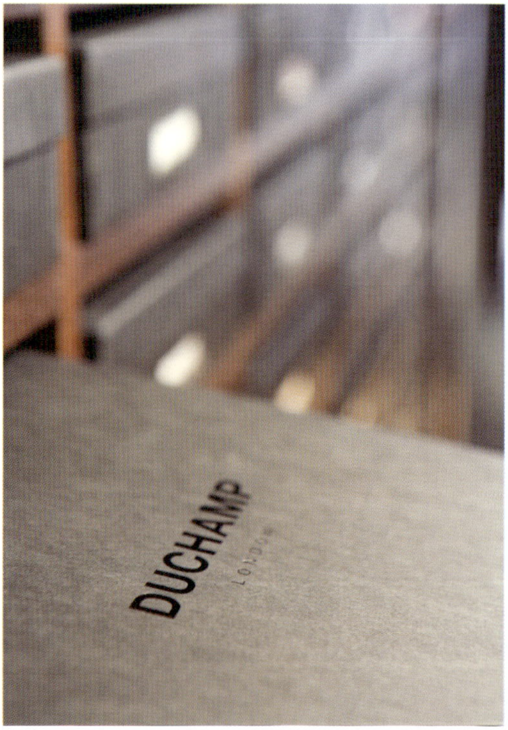
DUCHAMP
LONDON

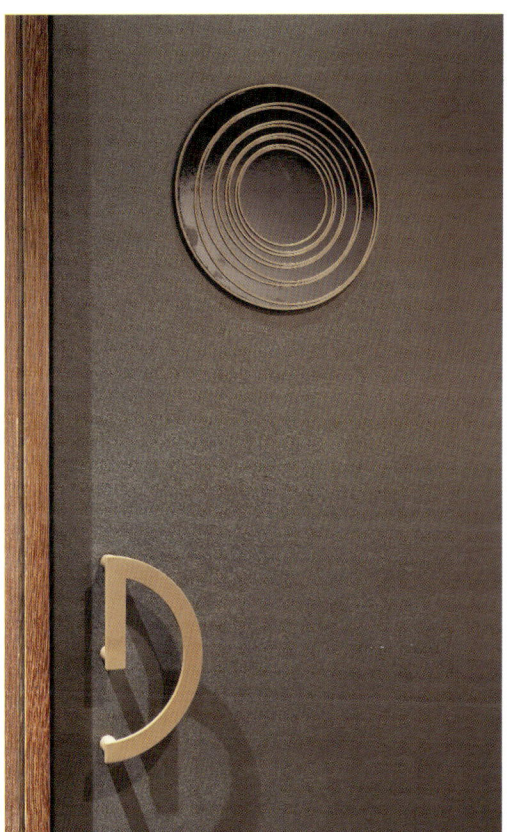

The refined logotype and new roundel motif are inspired by the visual experiments of Marcel Duchamp.

Institut Parfumeur Flores

Bunch, www.bunchdesign.com

Zagreb's Institut Parfumeur Flores is a shop, perfumery, and a little coffee place, all in one. Having an array of different pieces to brand for this new store's comprehensive identity, Bunch created a set of geometrical flowers. These can easily be used, in isolation or all together, to convey the brand and quickly identify it as belonging to the world of scents and perfumes.

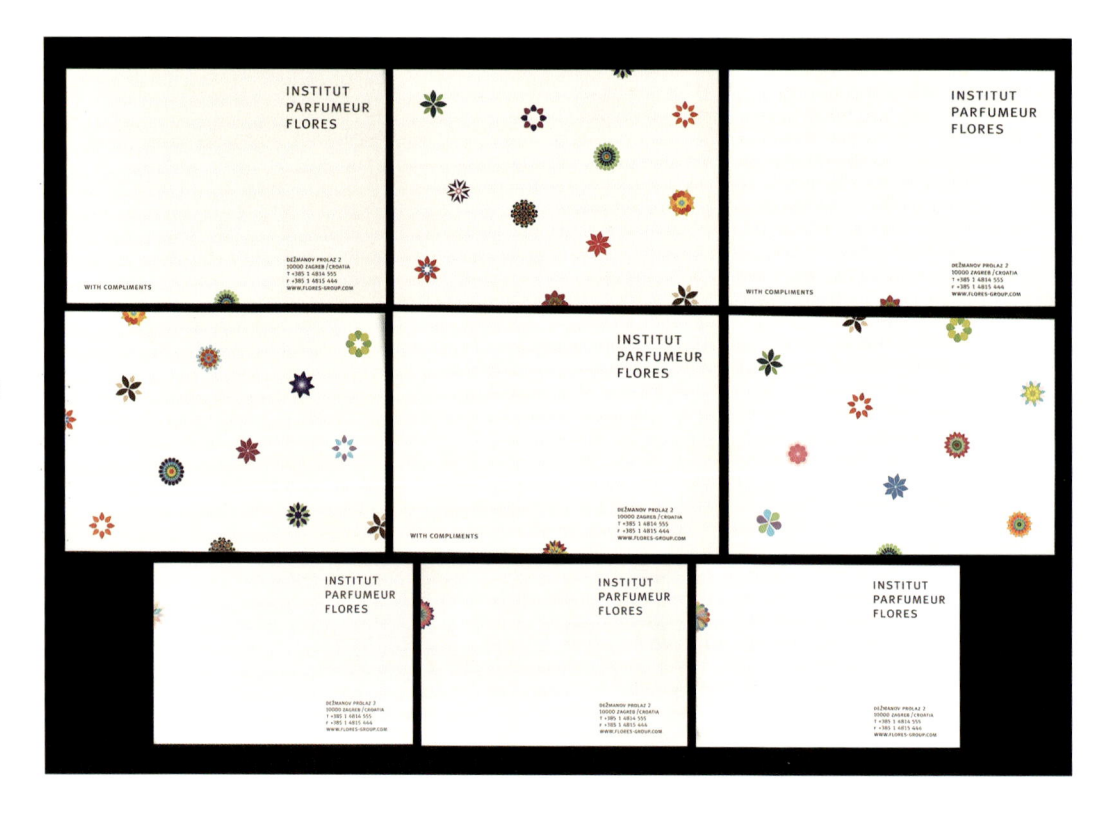

2 Dezmanov Prolaz
10000 Zagreb
Croatia
www.flores-group.com

Graphics on the store's façade depict the idea of an oasis environment amidst the urban concrete.

65

Foil-blocked store invites and promotional pencils given to costumers.

INSTITUT
PARFUMEUR
FLORES
INSTITUT
PARFUMEUR
FLORES

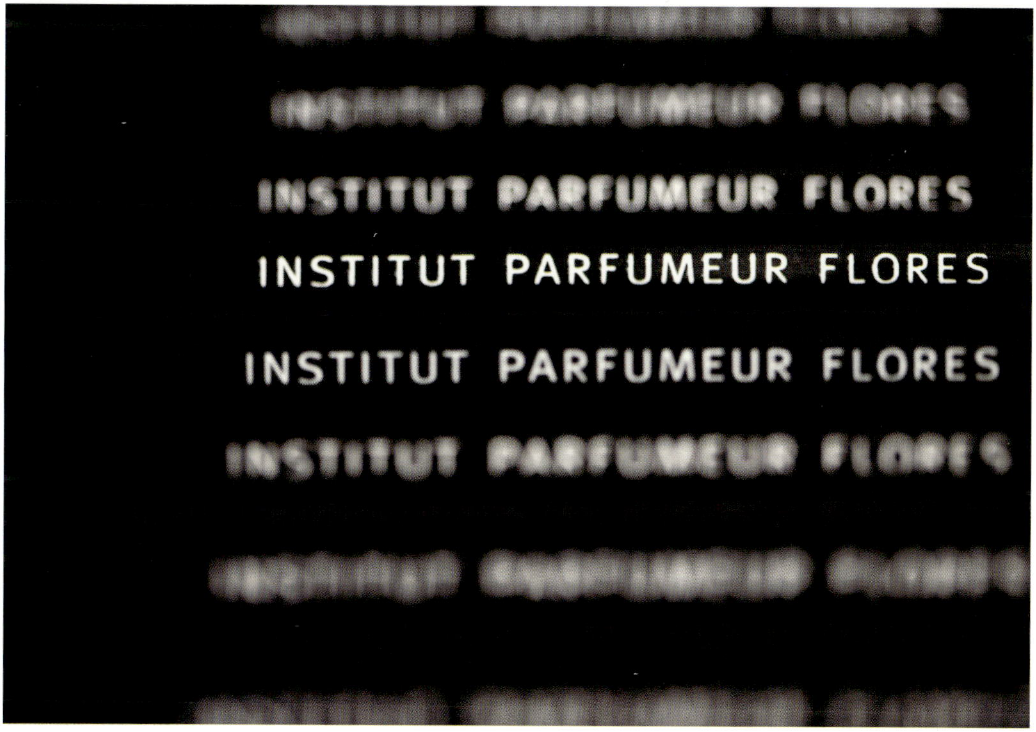
INSTITUT PARFUMEUR FLORES
INSTITUT PARFUMEUR FLORES
INSTITUT PARFUMEUR FLORES

The flower sets on stationery and cards; a slightly more psychedelic version adorns the notebooks.

INSTITUT
PARFUMEUR
FLORES

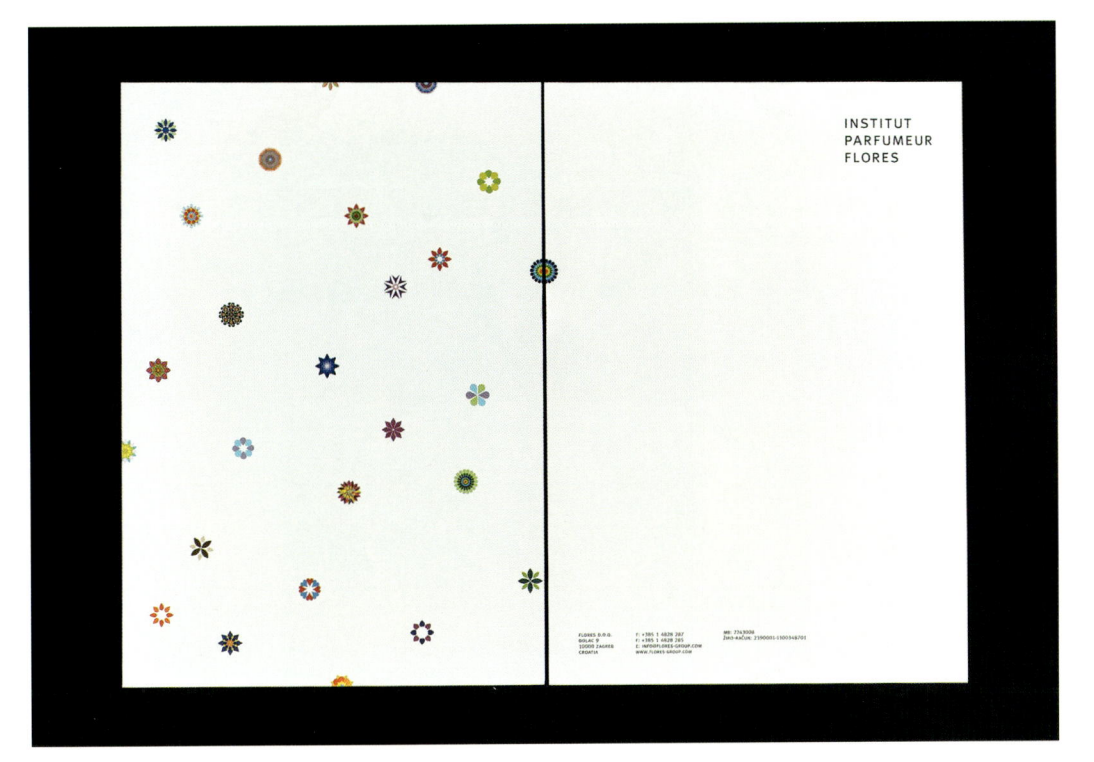

69

Zekka

Block Branding, www.blockbranding.com

Stocked with international experimental labels like Rick Owens, Raf Simons and Ann Demeulemeester, Zekka opened its doors on King Street to the pleasure of Perth's most fashion-forward men. Block Branding was responsible for developing the store's brand identity, taking their inspiration from curio cabinets and Victorian travel journals to create a sense of the exotic, intriguing and precious.

74-76 King Street
Perth, WA 6000
Australia
www.zekka.com

Matthews Architecture was in charge of designing Zekka's beautiful interiors.

ZEKKA

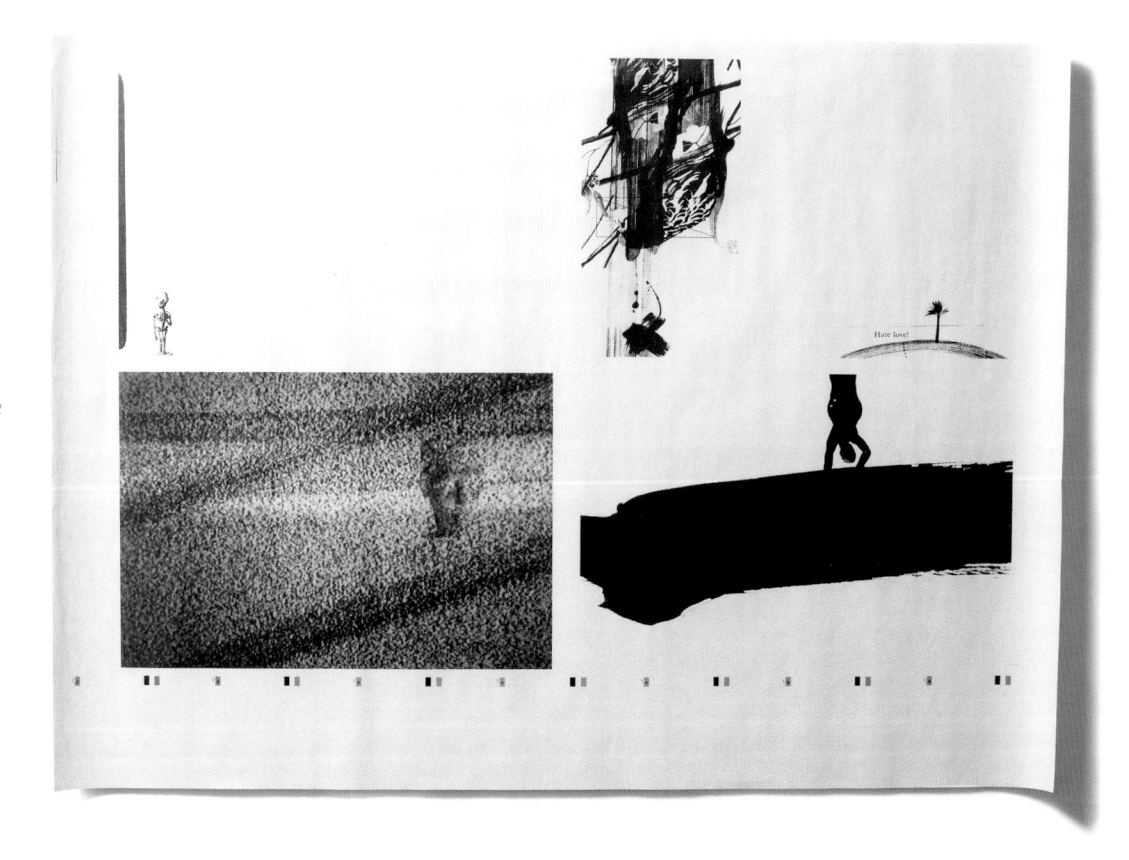

Wrapping paper and store launch invite. Invite illustration by Andrew Nicholls.

Birth

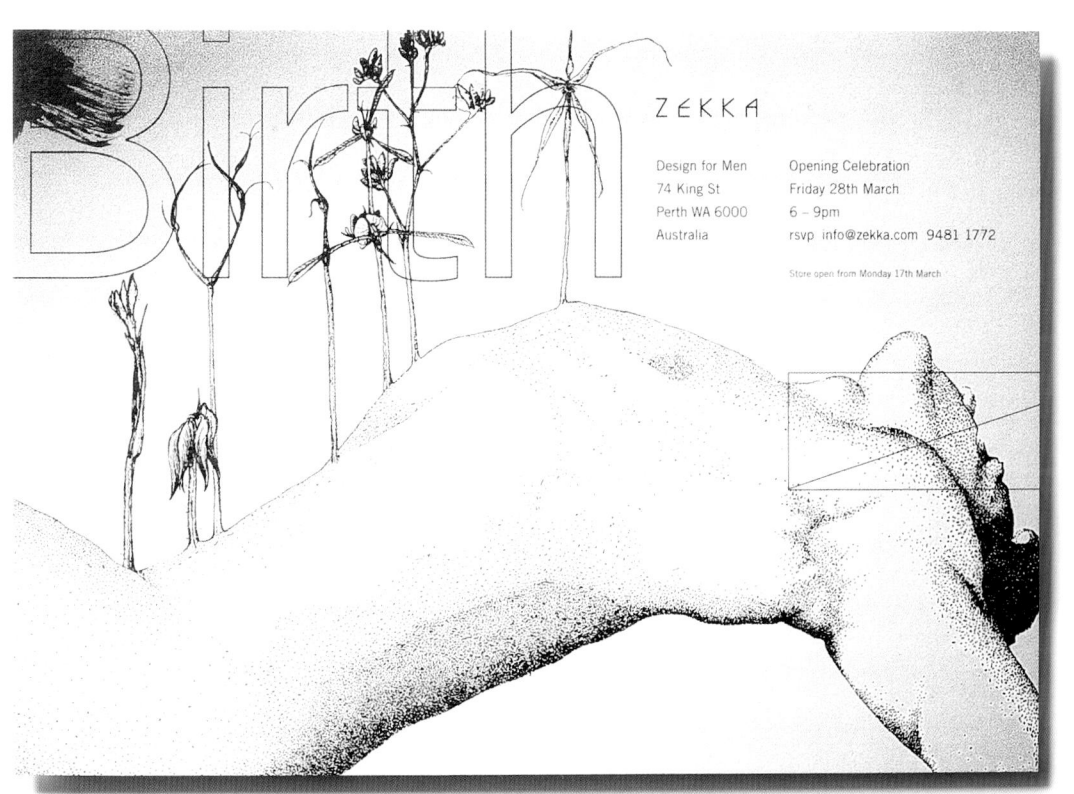

ZEKKA

Design for Men
74 King St
Perth WA 6000
Australia

Opening Celebration
Friday 28th March
6 – 9pm
rsvp info@zekka.com 9481 1772

Store open from Monday 17th March

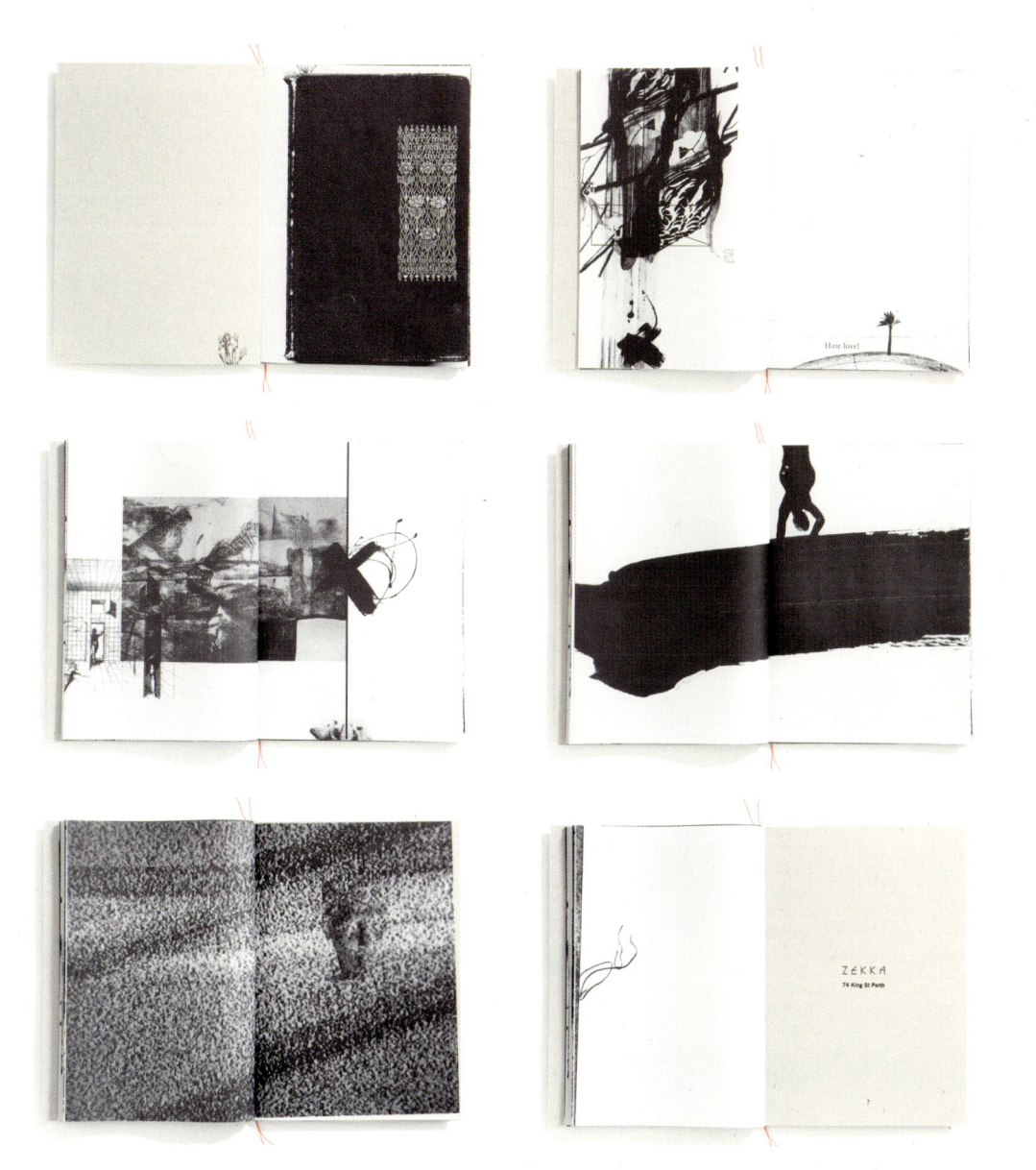

This limited-edition brochure created for the launch is a tactile journey into the mind of Zekka.

Hayford & Rhodes

Company, www.company-london.com

Building on the brand's classic British heritage, Company updated the Hayford & Rhodes identity by combining it with a fresh look that reflects the new owners' passion for design. Artist Farida El Gazzar was commissioned to paint illustrations of classic English flowers, which were then complemented with a simple typographic logo and carried across the packaging, stationery and corporate uniforms.

15 Queen Street
London EC4N 1TX
United Kingdom
www.hayfordandrhodes.co.uk

Hayford & Rhodes is London's oldest known florist and was founded in 1924.

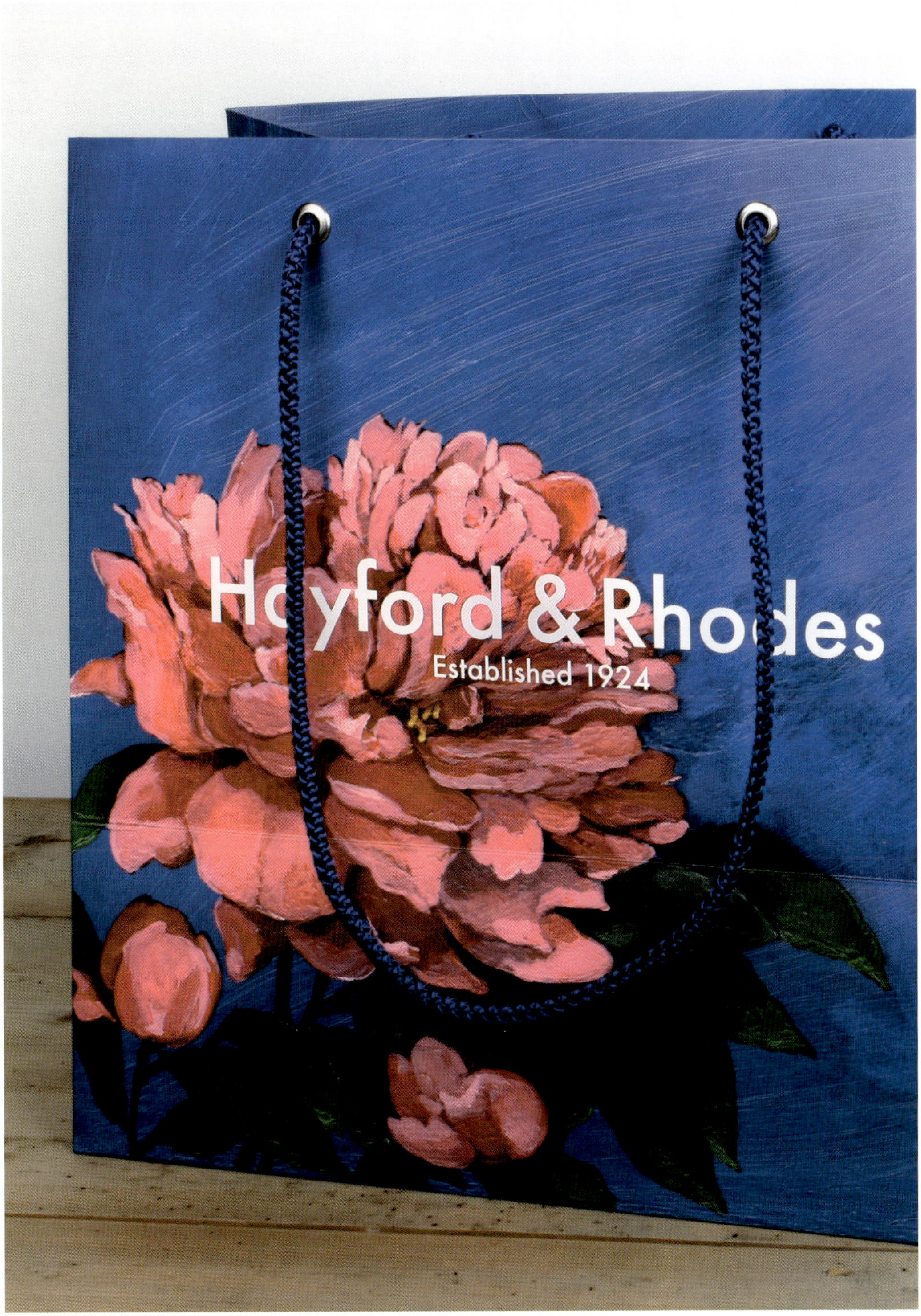
Hayford & Rhodes
Established 1924

78

Futura, a typeface designed in 1927, was chosen because of its classic yet timeless character.

Hayford & Rhodes
Established 1924

Hayford & Rhodes
Established 1924
Florist of Distinction
www.hayfordandrhodes.co.uk
T 020 7248 5312
Hayford & Rhodes
Established 1924
www.hayfordandrhodes.co.uk

His & Hers

Are Venus and Mars able to shop together in the same galaxy? Some shops and brands have made this possible by keeping a versatile character, using humor and pop culture instead of gender stereotypes and stocking the kind of design classics that make everyone happy: jeans, t-shirts and addictive limited-edition collectibles. Championing the kind of multi-faceted environment where polar opposites might come together, print and packaging identity pieces usually feature simple variations in size, shade and material to suit gender-specific items, while brand logos and color schemes remain to blur the lines.

Actually...

&Larry, www.andlarry.com

As the name of the store suggests, Actually... is constantly engaging in casual but honest banter with its clients – ever-changing and evolving in terms of topics and opinion. Singapore studio &Larry is in charge of the store's identity, and their conceptual carrier bags have become a hit item with customers. Below is the "baglet" model, which transforms into a singlet with a few snips of the scissors.

29 A Seah Street
Singapore 188385
Republic of Singapore
www.actually.com.sg

Suspended drawers and floating tables full of rare finds display Actually...'s handpicked merchandise.

83

An older series of carrier bags poked fun at their own popularity as limited collectible items.

85

These silver foil bags came with a set of cheeky slogan stickers to customize their look.

Actually...
Quit Staring!
Kiss My Ass!
I Can't Help It!
Actually...
Actually...
Actually...
Jeans, bags, tees & things
Paul Khor
www.actually.com.sg

Actually...
Jeans, bags, tees & things
Paul Khor
curator

Actually...
cos
We sell these brands
we look good in them
Freitag
Jerome Olivet
Fifth Avenue Shoe Repair
Federation
Hells Bells
Tretorn
Munich
Religion
Ksubi
GSUS
Elvis Jesus
AG Jeans
K Karl Lagerfeld
Queen of E.vil
Denim Design Lab
29A Seah Street (facing Raffles Hotel)
www.actually.com.sg

88

The "umbagla" carriers are both pretty and useful, with a second life as makeshift umbrellas.

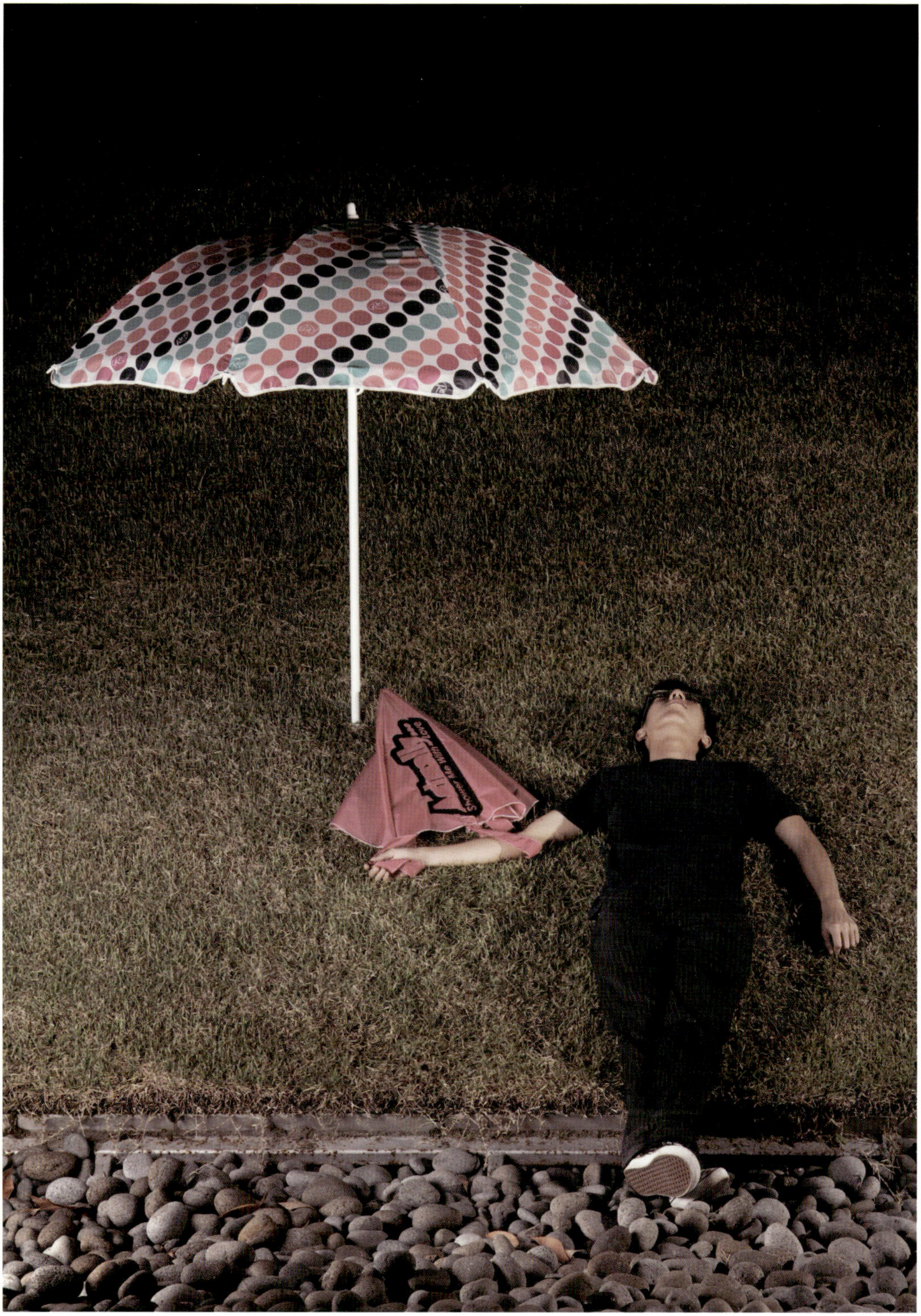

Greta & Luis

Nils Völker, www.nilsvoelker.de

Greta & Luis is a small chain of fashion stores located in Berlin, selling high-quality, casual and modern clothes. Nils Völker energized the new brand image, using a unique typeface and a corporate design that reflected the storeowner's philosophy. Illuminated signs, three different paper bags plus a plastic version used during sales, several print products and a website complete the identity.

Rosenthaler Straße 15
10119 Berlin
Germany
www.gretaundluis.com

The name Greta & Luis was chosen to point out that fashion is for both men and women.

91

Eins gleich vorweg:
Die guten Dinge bleiben:
die Atmosphäre, die
Menschen und die liebe-
volle Auswahl der Kollek-
tionen. Jedoch nach
sieben Jahren wird es Zeit
für einen Wechsel: Zwei
neue Läden sind dazu-
gekommen, und aus den
alten Namen Studio 08
und Studio 25 wird ein
neuer:
Greta & Luis
Wir finden das ist ein
guter Grund zu feiern und
möchten Sie herzlich dazu
einladen, am Freitag,
18. Juli ab 18.00 Uhr in
unserem neuen Laden,
in der Rosenthaler Str. 15
www.gretaundluis.com
Greta & Luis
Greta & Luis
Studio 25
Studio 25
Greta & Luis
Studio 25
Greta & Luis

Greta & Luis

The corporate design aims to be honest, straightforward and minimalist but remarkable in detail.

Levi's

Checkland Kindleysides, www.checklandkindleysides.com

The new concept for Levi's is based on their "Revolution" store design, which has been pared back to create a more minimal look – a blank canvas to which the core values of heritage, innovation and craftsmanship have been added. Checkland Kindleysides respected the spaces by restoring and renovating existing features of either historic or aesthetic relevance, such as the original flooring and wall finishes.

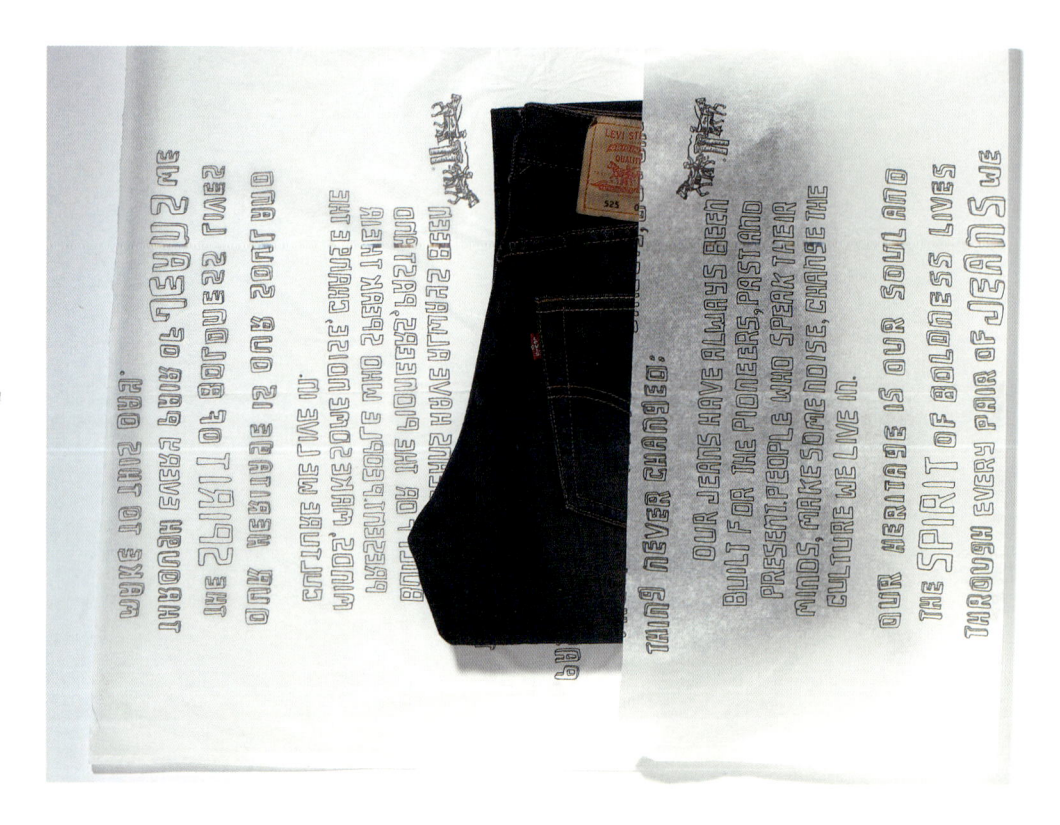

Kammenstraat 39
2000 Antwerp
Belgium
www.eu.levi.com

The new Levi's stores have a lighter atmosphere and a more unisex appeal.

95

96

Hanging displays set against wall drawings and the revisited classic carrier bags and packaging.

Neon signs, swing tags and custom signage are dotted around the area dedicated to the iconic 501 jeans.

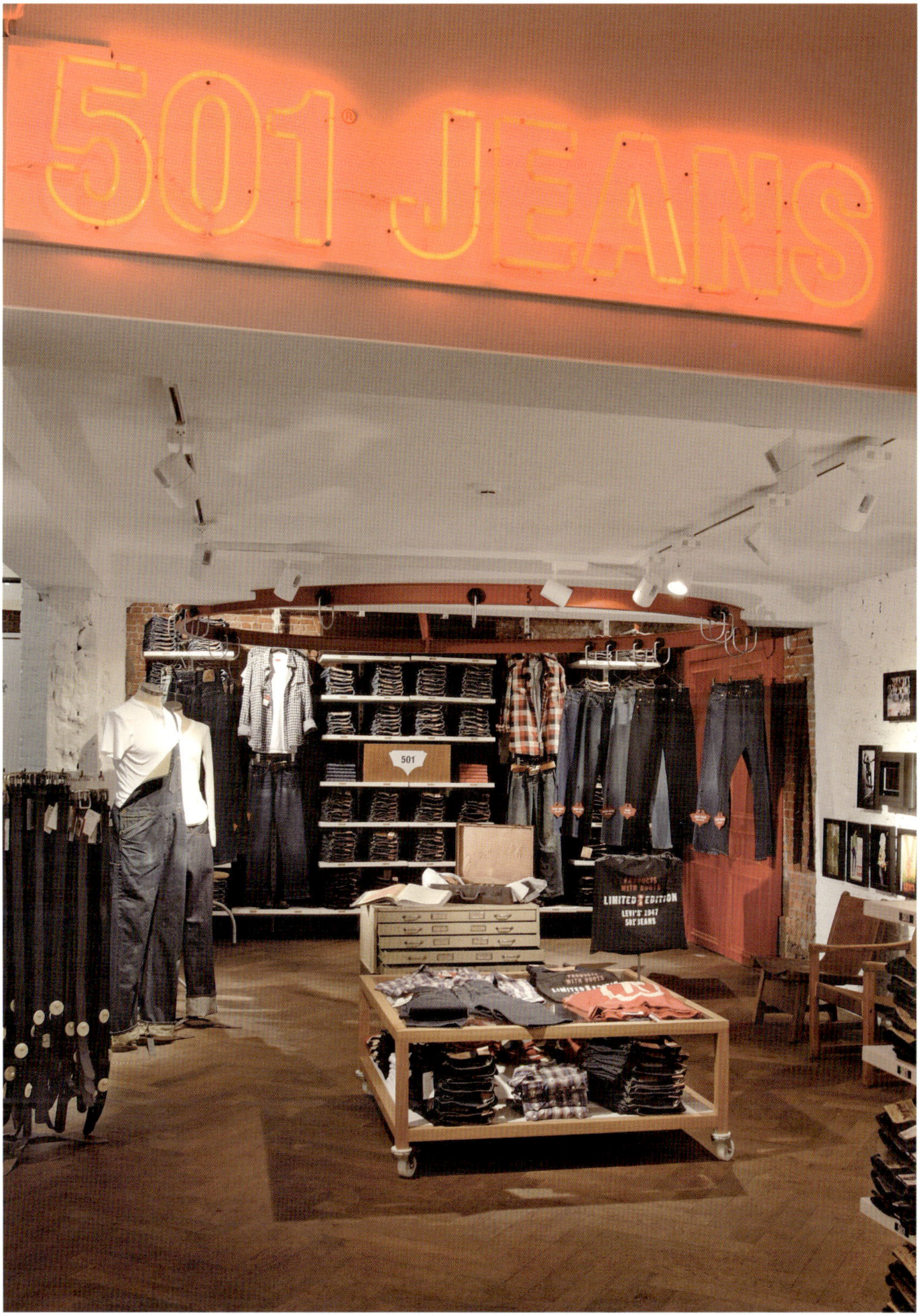
501® JEANS
501
LIMITED EDITION
LEVI'S® 1947
501® JEANS

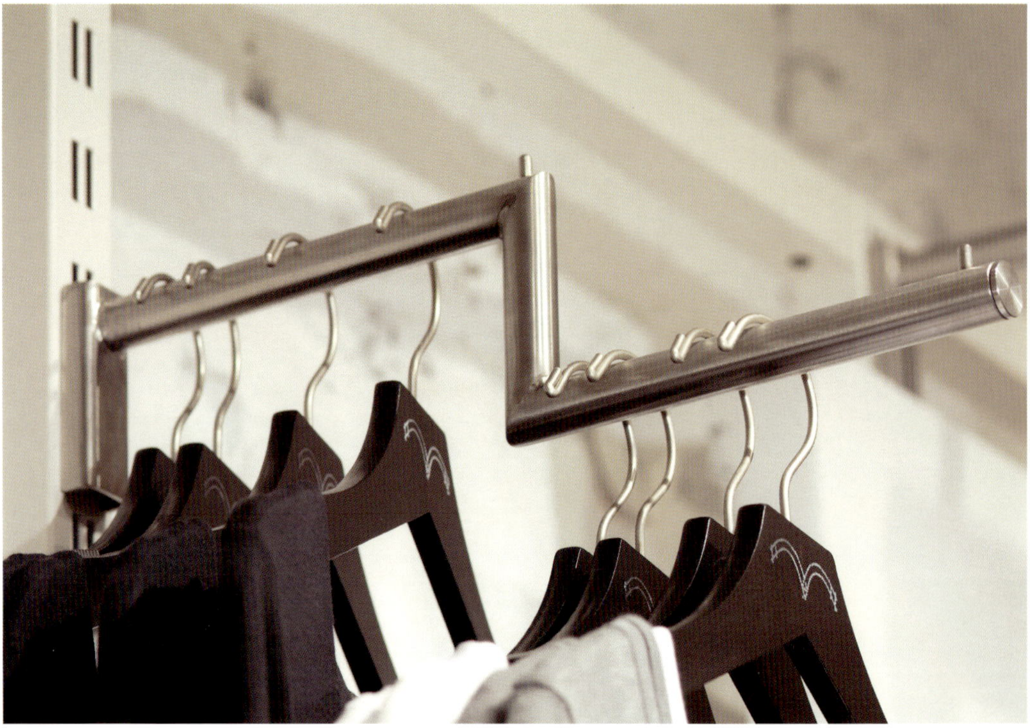

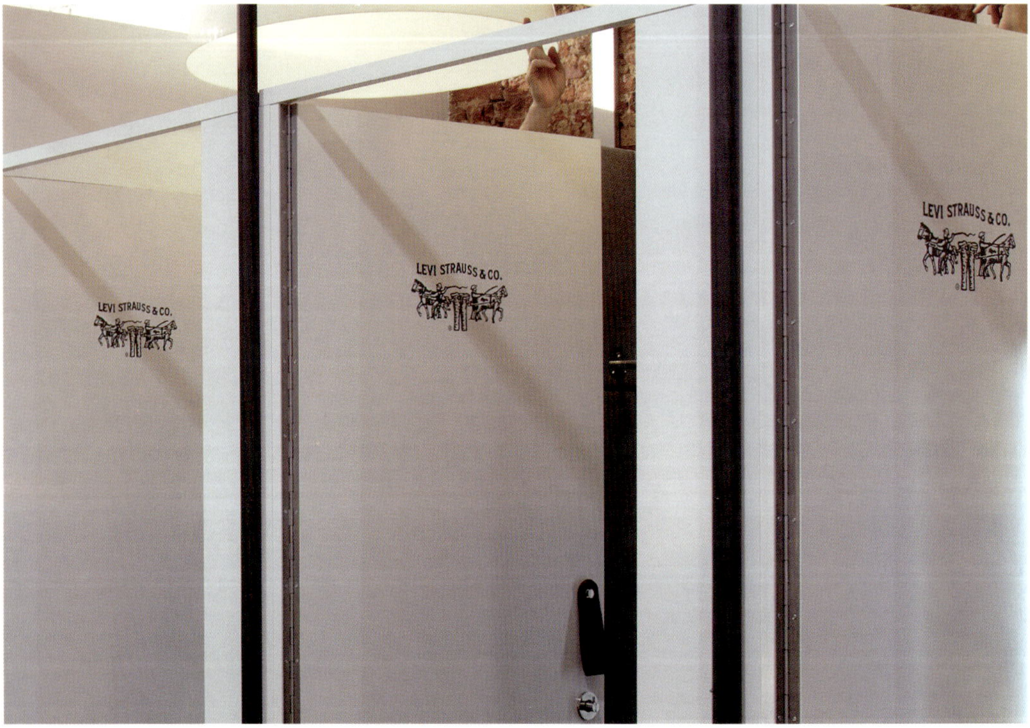
LEVI STRAUSS & CO.
LEVI STRAUSS & CO.
LEVI STRAUSS & CO.

Collections are merchandised against soft-whitewashed brick walls, giving prominence to the products.

Lovem

C100 Studio, www.c100studio.com

A multi-disciplinary design studio, C100 Studio works on various projects involving creative direction, graphic design and illustration. In the case of Lovem, a small German clothing label, the corporate image was kept to a minimal style, with single labels usable for all sizes of garments, thanks to a coded system, while technicolor graphics were unleashed for the t-shirt designs.

Available at Spielbar Tragbar
Klenzestrasse 54
80469 München
Germany
www.getlovem.com

Easy-to-wear t-shirts in a variety of bold designs are the main crowd-pleasers at Lovem.

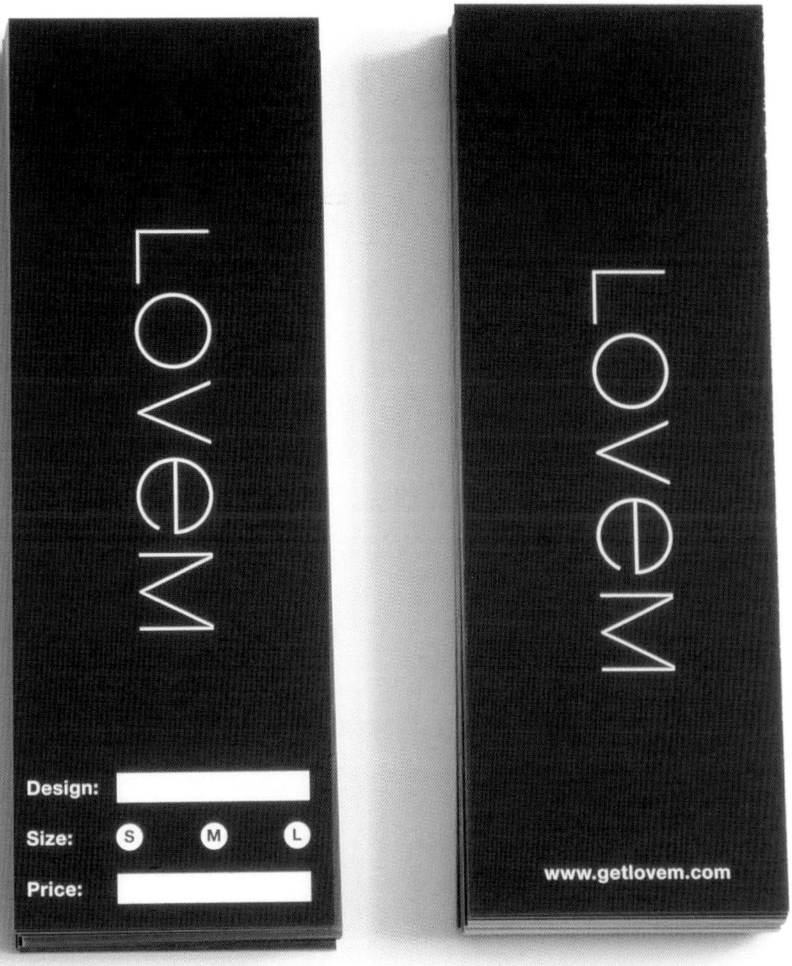
LOVEM
Design:
Size: S M L
Price:
LOVEM
www.getlovem.com

104

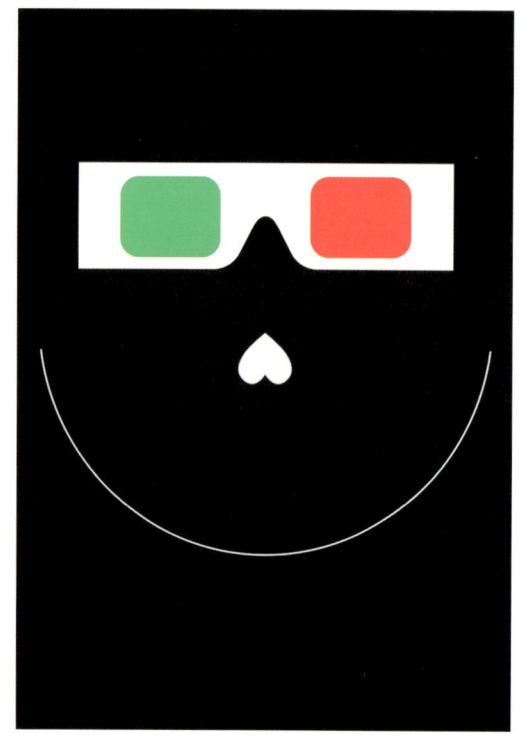

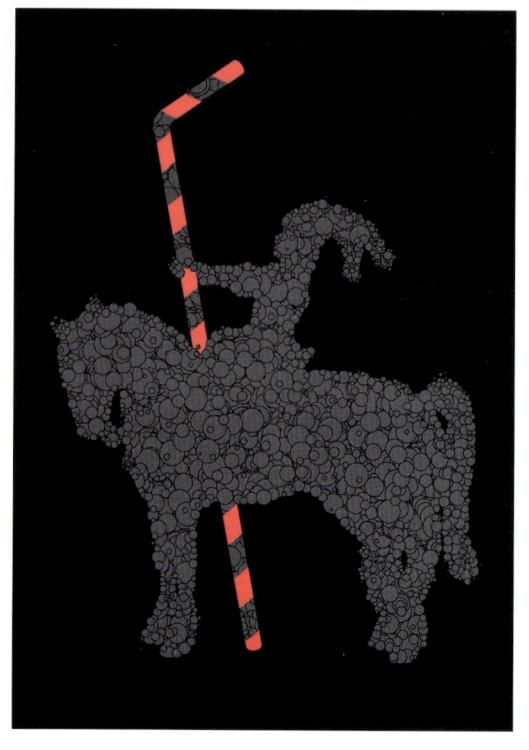

Flyers are reminiscent of Polaroid photographs, while primary colors adorn cheerful t-shirt designs.

105

PARISTEXAS

Scandinavian DesignLab, www.scandinaviandesignlab.com

An exclusive boutique in the heart of Copenhagen, PARISTEXAS has a store collection composed of international trendsetting brands. Scandinavian DesignLab's assignment involved creating an identity that supported a sense of unique, limited and underground exclusivity. Strange hybrid creatures crawl over tags, large-sized posters and labels, inviting visitors into a secret avant-garde world.

Krystalgade 18-20
Copenhagen 1172
Denmark
www.paristexas.dk

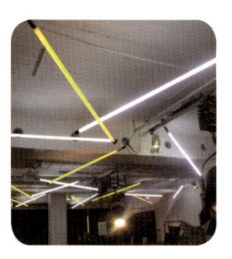

Futuristic neon fixtures mingle with stage lighting in the store's interior.

107

Packaging designs for limited-edition t-shirts, gold foil-blocked business cards and store notebooks.

109

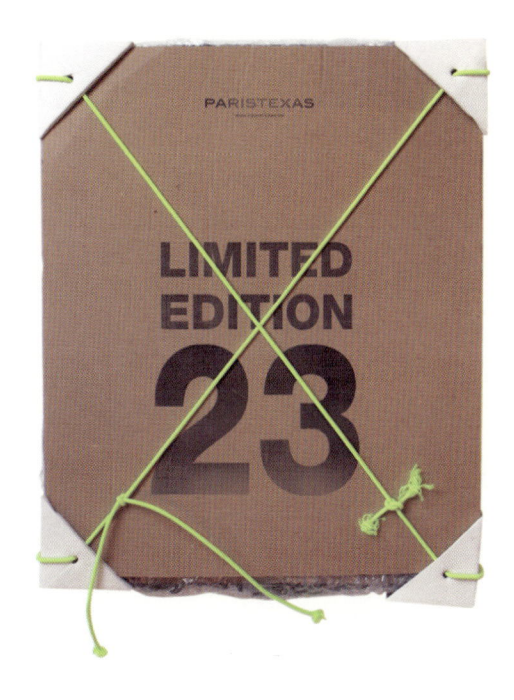

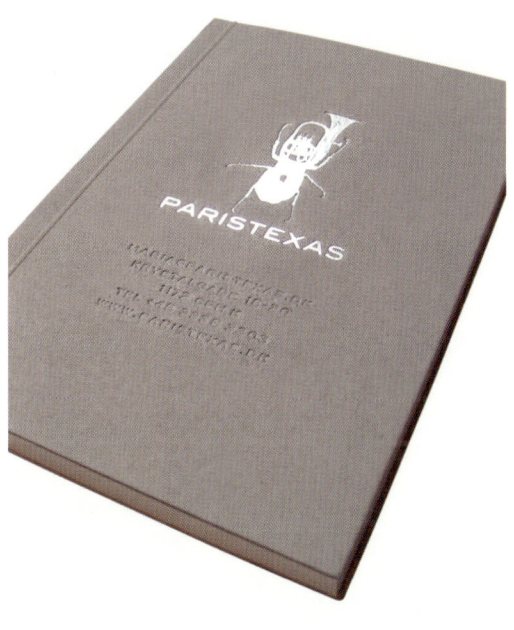

Grand
opening
PARISTEXAS
Paristexas slår dørene op for første gang torsdag d.14 december ! Vi inviterer derfor til reception fra kl. 17.00 - 21.00 i den nye butik på Krystalgade 18-20, 1172 Kbh.K., hvor butikken vil være åben og vi serverer champagne og musik.
Vi glæder os til at se dig.
Butikken vil gennem den kommende tid løbende præsentere kollektioner fra følgende designere: Martin Margiela / Neil Barett / Junya Watanabe / Tsumori chisato / Sportmax Deflé / Emma Cook / Aquascutum / RAF by Raf Simons / Rick Owens / Tsubi / Karen Walker / Number (n)ine / Undercover / Earnest Sewn / Kenzo Minami / James Perse / Juicy Couture / Burfitt / Collection Privée / Mosslight / BlueBlood / J.Lindeberg / Lara Bohinc

The logotype is simple and taut, while the color palette is flexible and changes with the collections.

NEW SHOP
Proudly presents
2007 Fashion collections from:

Martin Margiela / Junya Watanabe / Sportmax Defilé / J.Lindeberg / Zucca / Aquascutum / Rick Owens
Undercover / RAF by Raf Simons / Kenzo Minami / Juicy Couture / Surface2Air / BlueBlood / Neil Barrett
Collection Priveé / Tsumori Chisato / Emma Cook / Charles Anastase / Lara Bohinc / James Perse / Burfitt
Earnest Sewn / Tsubi / Mosslight / Number (n)ine

PARISTEXAS
KRYSTALGADE 18-20 / 1172 KBH K / 3336 3303
WWW.PARISTEXAS.DK

A fusion of instruments and earthly insects symbolizes the store's symphony of underground collections.

113

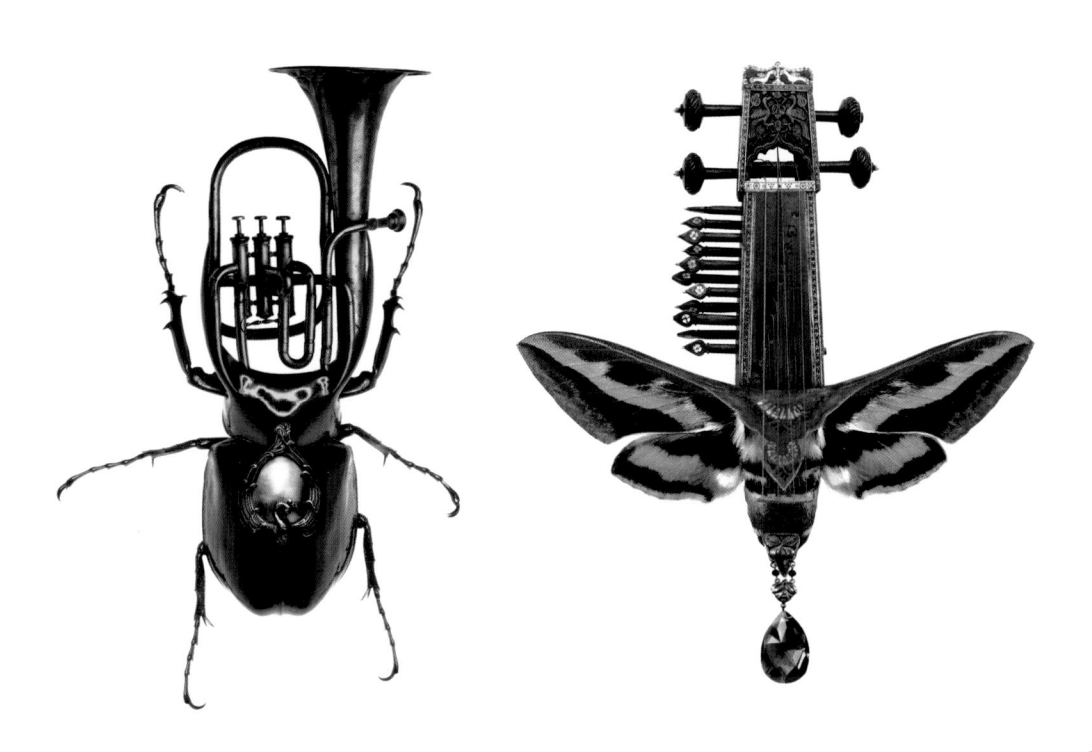

Wooonderland

&Larry, www.andlarry.com

A new experimental retail playground where the silly, happy, playful and – most of all – stylish rule, Wooonderland is another concept venture by the people behind Actually... The logo is deliberately big and bold, and the color palette is composed of bright primary colors, expressing the personality of the boutique as well as manifesting the kind of merchandise it carries.

2nd Floor Unit 10
Wheelock Place
501 Orchard Road
Singapore 238880
Republic of Singapore
www.wooonderland.com

Wooonderland's oversized logos give the boutique the aura of a comic book hero's secret hideout.

KEEP TRIPPIN'
MY BLUE
GENUINE QUALITY MADE IN J.P.N.
W
L
ROUTE 503

What's the point of fashion if you can't have some fun with it.

WOOONDERLAND

Dr Denim Jeansmaker, Edwin, Something by Edwin, 55DSL, RVCA, Local Celebrity, Crooked Monkey, Airbag Craftworks, LaGa, Stuff, Ductbill, Capsul & more to come.

#02-10 Wheelock Place, Singapore
tel 67380002   www.wooonderland.com

Bags come with a larger version of the "clip" store card and swing along with customer's movements.

The logo links to the owner's other store (Actually…) through the use of the ellipsis.

WOOONDERLAND

COME PLAY WITH OUR THINGS!

WOOONDERLAND

AIRBAG CRAFTWORKS
DR DENIM JEANSMAKER
EDWIN
RVCA
CAPSUL
DUCTBILLS
POKETO
LOCAL CELEBRITY
55DSL
THREADLESS
STUFF
& MORE!

#02-10 WHEELOCK PLACE, SINGAPORE   WWW.WOOONDERLAND.COM

WOOONDERLAND CELEBRATES SINGAPORE DESIGN FESTIVAL! GET **30% OFF** AIRBAG CRAFTWORKS ONLY WHEN YOU FLASH US THIS PAGE. OFFER VALID TILL 16 DEC 2007.

Snack Attack

Whether touting chocolate-covered bonbons or organically-grown local greens, food retailers wishing to attract customers know that an appealing presentation of their edible goods is half the battle won. Elements vindicating the gastronomic culture surrounding the foods give another dimension to the basic necessity of eating, while comforting notions of family tradition and the "homemade" reassure the buyers on their choice. Snacks and dried foods are easily packaged, carried and stored, and make an ideal product to showcase beautiful packaging series with tasty variations and display potential.

Afro Coffee

The President, www.thepresident.co.za

The picture of a new, young and creative Africa, Afro Coffee is a place where you can drink single-origin coffee, buy young African fashion labels and even African art. Most importantly, however, you can take the coffee and the original tea blends home with you. In-store furnishings and decoration are produced in the townships, thereby creating employment, and the branding is designed by The President design studio.

Bürgerspitalplatz 5
5020 Salzburg
Austria
www.afrocoffee.com

The logo, designed by The President, has its roots in a barbershop poster, a universal element in Afro culture.

123

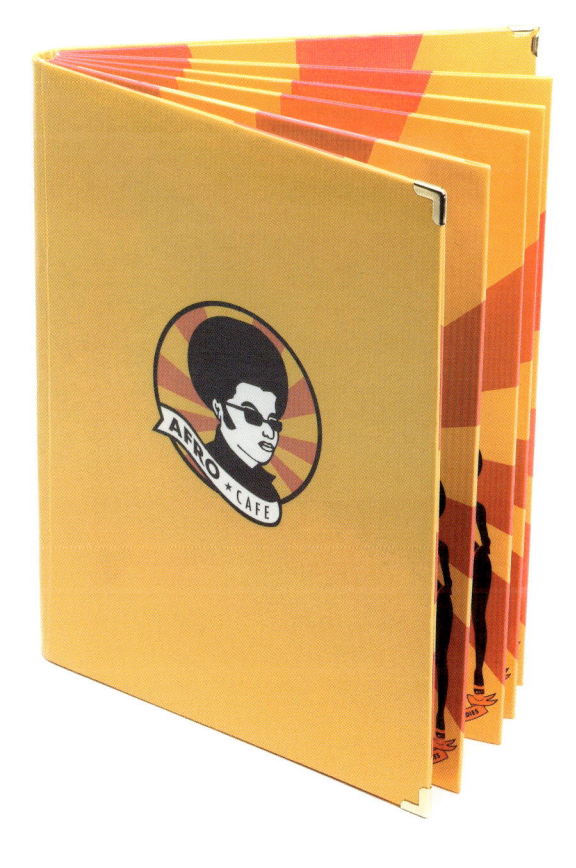

124

The sum of Afro culture creativity is presented at the Afro Cafes – bright and self-confident.

Natcha

Estudio Rosa Lazaro, www.rlazaro.com

Founded in Barcelona in 1958 as an initiative from a young go-ahead couple, Isidre and Rosa, today the Natcha confectionery is an innovative company that is still clearly going for quality and constant improvements in terms of both product and service. Estudio Rosa Lazaro was enlisted to design a new logo and matching graphic applications for the packaging and commercial space.

Av. Sarrià, 45
08029 Barcelona
Spain
www.natcha.cat

Natcha makes quality products following the crafts of the baking tradition.

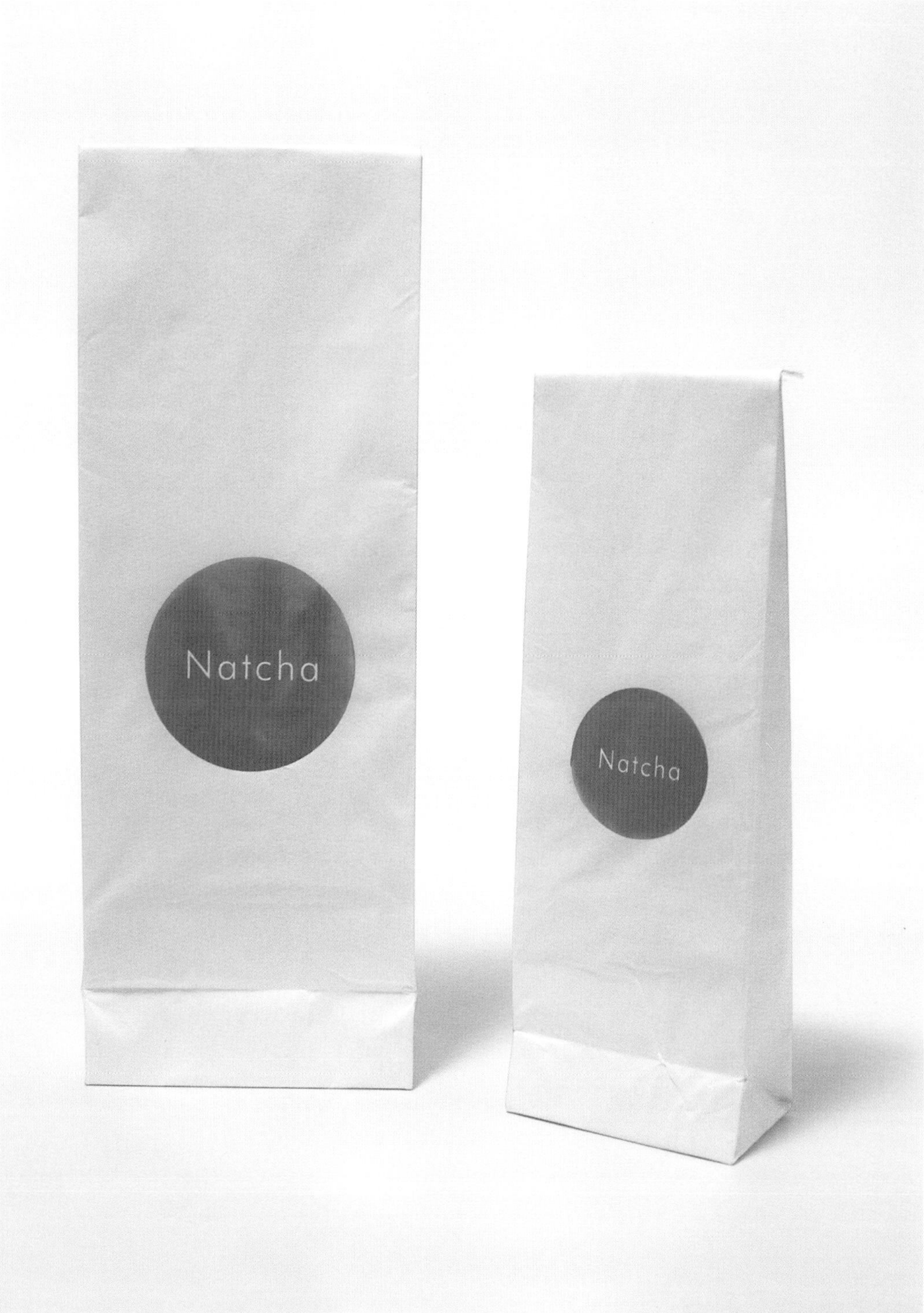
Natcha
Natcha

Uniforms in dark chocolate hues keep it simple and professional.

129

130

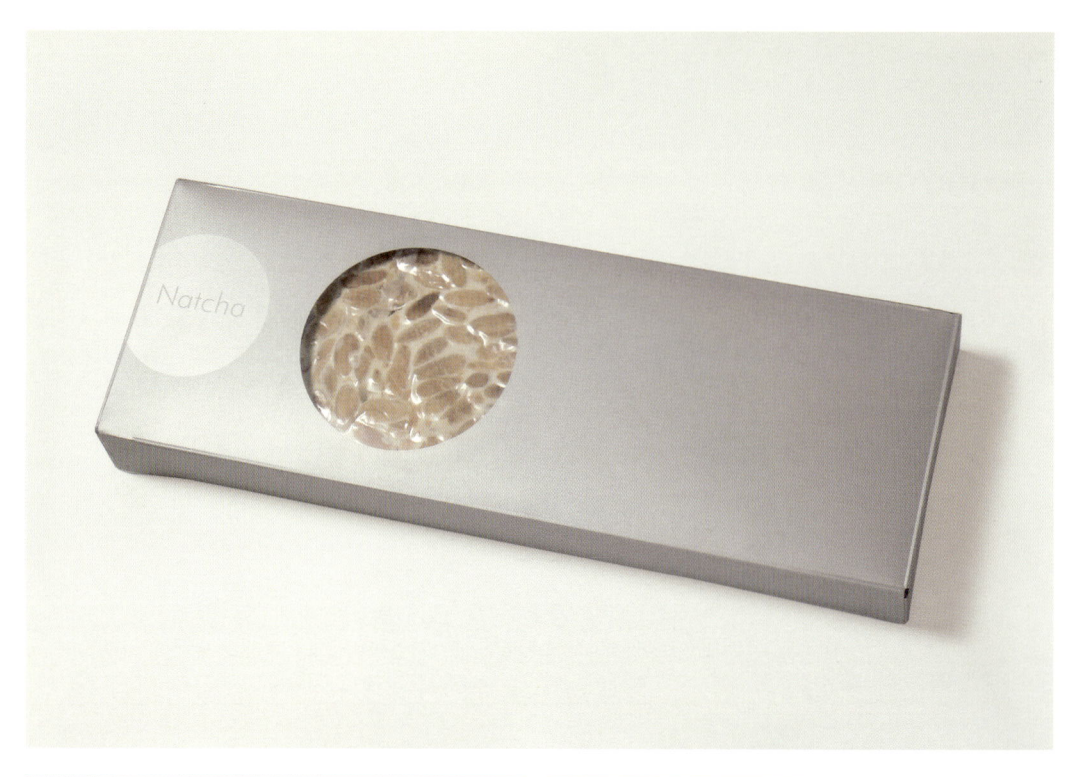

The circle logo is echoed in stickers, cut-outs and textured applications on in-store glass surfaces.

Unpackaged

Multistorey, www.multistorey.net

A company that sells produce without packaging, Unpackaged uses a self-serve system to eliminate wasteful packaging and its associated costs. Multistorey tackled the challenge of branding a package-less brand and designed a classic jar-shaped logo that can be found in various subtle applications throughout the shop: troughs containing the produce, gold vinyl window signage and shop cards.

42 Amwell Street
London EC1R 1XT
United Kingdom
www.beunpackaged.com

Shop invitations were foil-stamped directly onto recycled and cut-up boxes of cereal and detergent.

133

The four-step instructional diagram uses the rounded jar logo to inform the drawing style of other icons.

FILL

WEIGH

2.00

PAY

HOW IT WORKS

1. FILL YOUR
   CONTAINER
2. WE WEIGH
3. YOU PAY

RE-USE YOUR
OWN CONTAINER
& SAVE 50p

SAVE

Cacao Sampaka

Pati Núñez i Associats, www.patinunez.com

When asked to take part in the development and definition of the identity for a new branch of cocoa-themed shops, chocolate addict Pati Núñez dove in headfirst to bring back the historic cult of the mighty pod. The phrase she established as the brand philosophy was "The Culture of Cocoa," and the brand identity is based on investigating the traditional tasting of chocolate throughout time.

Consell de Cent, 292
08007 Barcelona
Spain
www.cacaosampaka.com

The open and accessible style of the product display is based on a produce market environment.

137

138

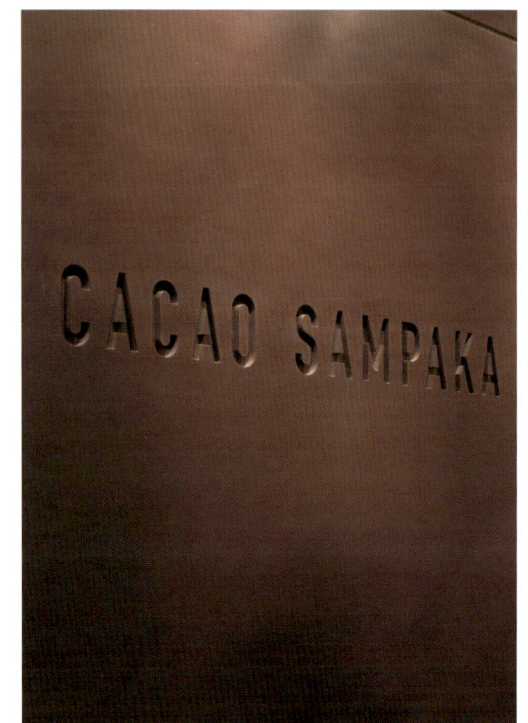

Photography works as an element of easy visual identification, as well as seduction and emotion.

140

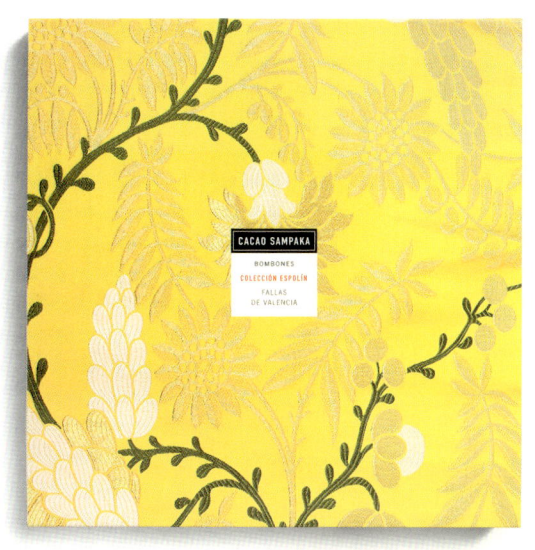

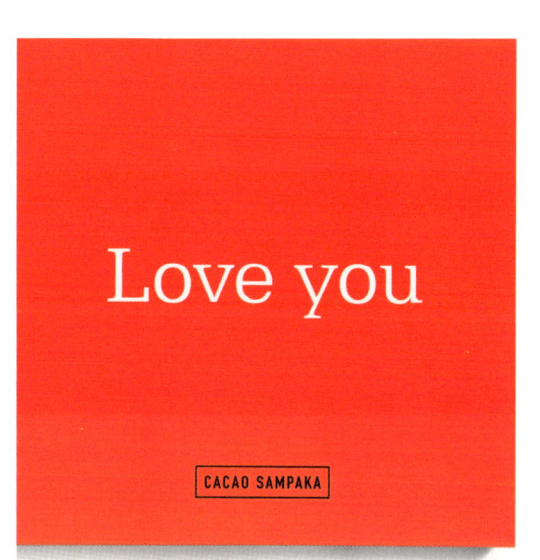

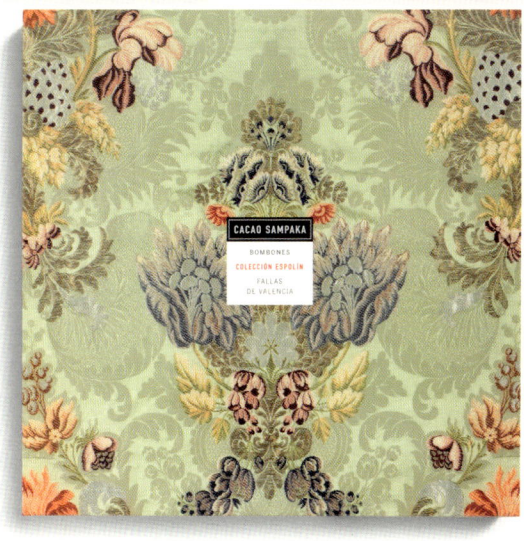

Special designs for Valentine's Day and Les Falles, a traditional Spanish celebration.

CACAO SAMPAKA

BOMBONES 70% CACAO

LA JOYA
TABASCO, MÉXICO

CACAO CRIOLLO BLANCO

The higher-range packaging is inspired by a rare species of cocoa nicknamed "porcelain."

CACAO SAMPAKA

CHOCOLATE NEGRO
70% CACAO

LA JOYA
TABASCO, MÉXICO

CACAO CRIOLLO
BLANCO

The Larder

Company, www.company-london.com

From signage to wallpaper and sugar bags, Company design studio developed a distinctive identity for this modern British delicatessen in London's Clerkenwell district. Drawing inspiration from traditional British values and aesthetics, the studio used a simple serif typeface for the logo, supported by a versatile ornamental pattern, in order to create a look that is classic yet contemporary.

91-93 St John Street
London EC1M 4NU
United Kingdom
www.thelarderrestaurant.com

The Larder is an open-all-day restaurant, bakery and take-away delicatessen shop.

145

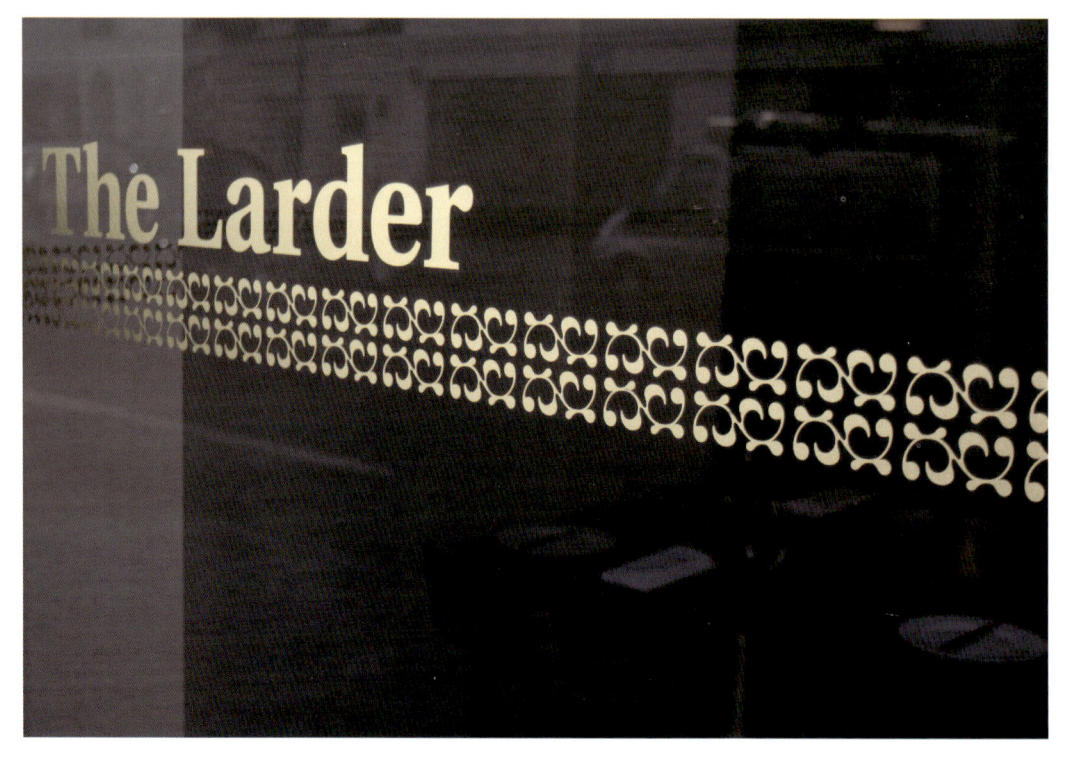

The Larder

A rich gold and deep eggplant color scheme was used for the pattern applications and wallpaper.

Pamper, Adorn & Indulge

The beauty process channeled by these shops starts with feeling great about your body and self. Botanically-enhanced body products and holistic skincare adopt soothing textures and imagery, while slicked chrome makeup packaging evokes futuristic beauty technology. The pampered body can then be adorned with either comfortable cotton briefs or deliciously naughty froufrous and accessorized with equally naughty toys, idiosyncratic jewels to reveal your soul or arts and craft pieces to please the mind.

Korres

k2 design, www.k2design.gr

A Greek company with roots in the first homeopathic pharmacy of Athens, Korres Natural Products has landed in typically stylish fashion in the grand Opera neighborhood of Paris. The new store, with its characteristically Parisian façade, winks to the brand's trademark aesthetics, building on Korres's design philosophy, which is based on contrasts. Packaging by Hélène Prablanc and K2 design.

13-15, rue Taitbout
75009 Paris
France
www.korres.com

Fans can instantly pick up the brand's iconic elements while also being surprised by new ones.

151

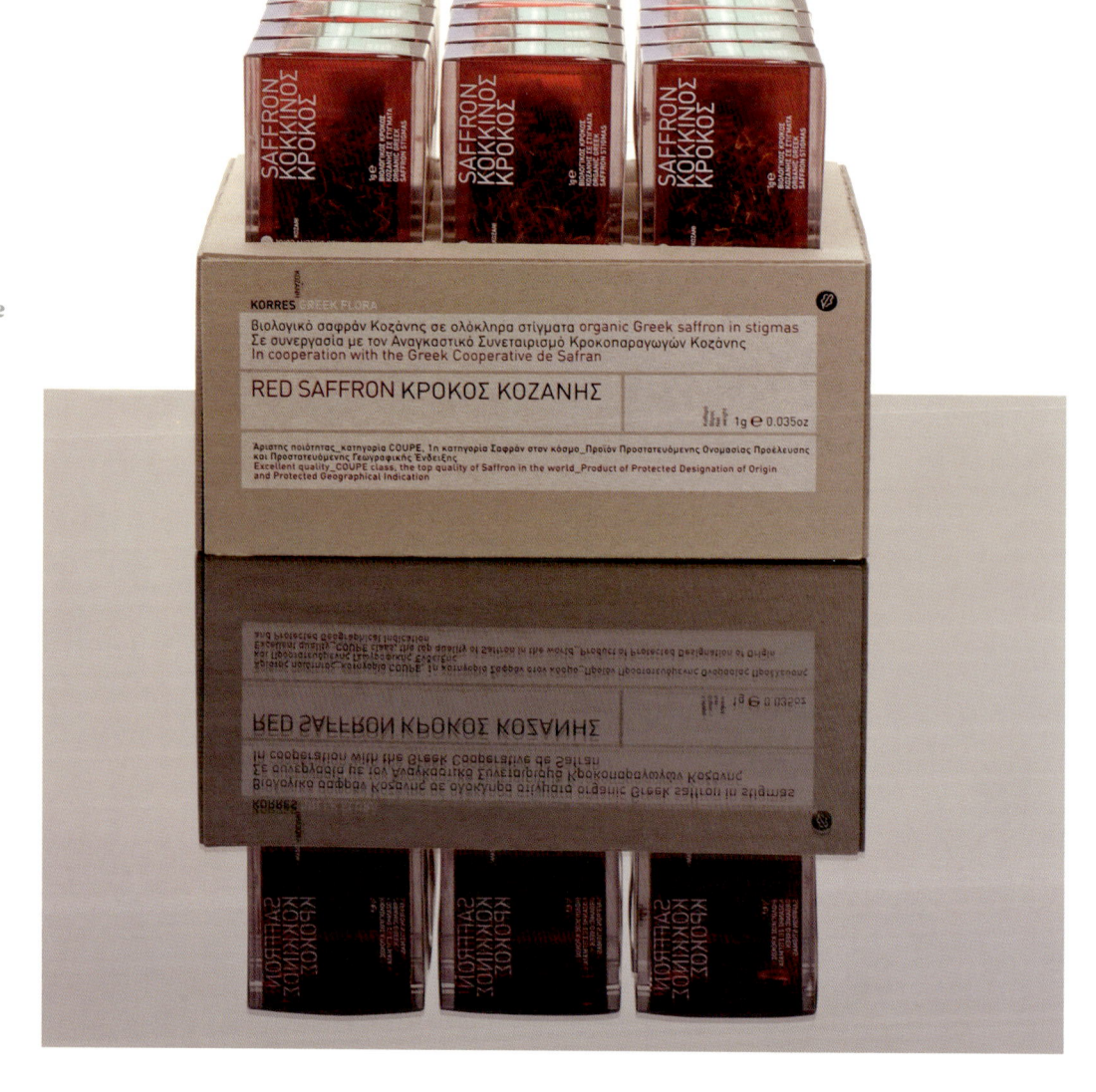

Item-specific display boxes bear explanatory labels; carrier bags mix plastic and wax paper.

I ♡ KORRESNATURALPRODUCTS

KORRES

ATHENS
LONDON
NEW YORK
TOKYO
GLASGOW
BARCELONA
MADRID
HELSINKI
PARIS
FRANKFURT
BEIJING
ISTANBUL

From homeopathic remedies to natural products

Korres natural products is a Greek company with roots in the first Homeopathic Pharmacy of Athens. The first Korres product was an aromatic herbal syrup with honey and aniseed, a recipe inspired by "rakomelon", a warming spirit-with-honey concoction, which George Korres' grandfather used to favour in his hometown on the island of Naxos. The company today offers more than 500 skin and hair care products, at leading department stores and 20 stand alone stores, in 28 countries around the world. **Our values** Korres natural products are based on 4 fundamental principles: • Naturally derived, top quality active ingredients. • Clinically tested effectiveness with no inflated promises. • Pleasing to the senses. • Reasonably priced to enable every-day use. **The syntheses** There are four types of active herbal ingredients that we use in our syntheses: • Unique herbs of the Greek flora, known for their traditional use: Olive oil, Thymus Honey, Basil, Camomile, Fennel, Sage, Linden, Rosemary, Mastiha • Medicinal herbs (our pharmacy heritage): Aloe vera, St John's Wort, Evening Primrose, Rosa Moschata, Thyme, Calendula, Echinacea, Gingo biloba, Ginseng, Hamamelis • New advanced herbal ingredients, Imperata cylindrica, Sunflower • Food ingredients, incorporated in their natural form into the formulas in order to maintain their properties: real edible Yoghurt and thyme Honey. At the same time we are committed to continuously developing the base of our products using technology and research in more environment friendly and skin-compatible ways. Thus, we broadly avoid the use of specific synthetic compounds like petroleum derived mineral oils, silicones, propylene glycol, ethanolamines, ammonia etc), replacing them with naturally derived ingredients, such as vegetable oils and aminoacids, that have nourishing properties and are friendly to the skin. **Our cooperations** in cooperation with the sector of Pharmacognosy (Pharmaceutics department, University of Athens), we participate in industrial research development programmes, with the object of utilising herbs of the Greek flora. At the same time, in cooperation with the Chios Mastiha Growers Association we have developed a special product line, based on Mastiha, the invaluable and unique resin of Chios. Moreover, in cooperation with the Cooperative de Safran, we have undertaken the responsibility to create an extensive range of products with Krokos Kozanis, the highest quality existing Saffron

153

White and black are the dominant colors both in the new Parisian Korres store and in the men's line press kit.

155

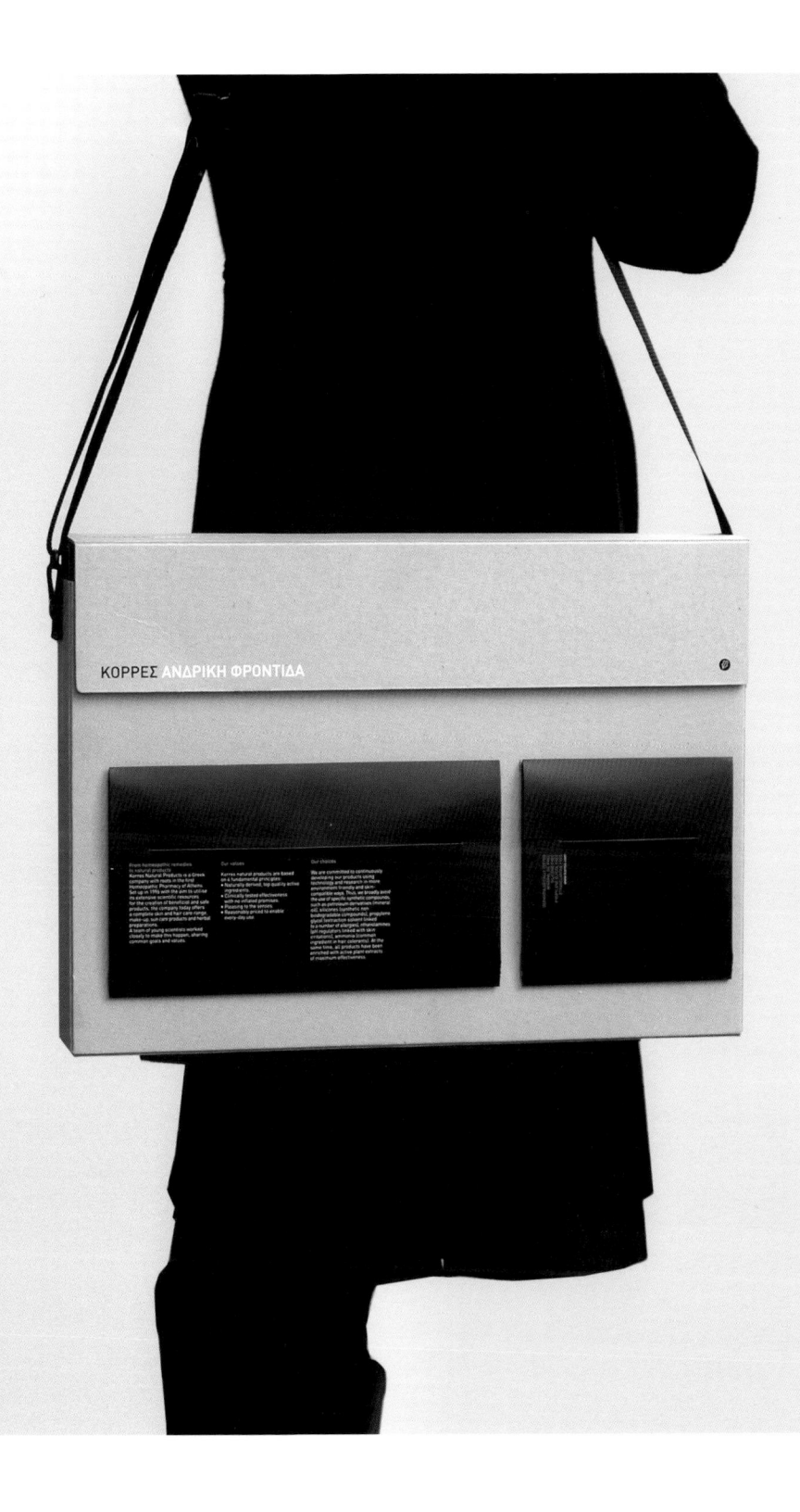

156

The brand's pharmaceutical resources in herbal preparations influenced the packaging graphics.

Tatty Devine

Tatty Devine, www.tattydevine.com

Having spawned an army of imitators in the recent years, Tatty Devine is the real deal when it comes to colorful and irreverent, plastic-fantastic charm jewelry and accessories. Fantastically elaborate pieces are set off in simple black debossed and foil-stamped boxes. Store cards come in various shapes, including playing cards, and window displays are on the highly imaginative side.

236 Brick Lane
Tower Hamlets
London E2 7EB
United Kingdom
www.tattydevine.com

Dynamic duo Rosie Wolfenden and Harriet Vine are the creators behind Tatty Devine's products.

159

Alternative carrier bags, heart-shaped gift tags and some masking tape featuring classic 3D glasses.

161

162

A spot of retro charm adorns the storefront and sidewalk outside the shop.

Tatty Devine

OPEN EVERY DAY
11 - 6 pm
WWW.TATTYDEVINE.COM
Soho shop at
57B Brewer Street, W1
020 7434 2257

Lascivious

Lascivious and Marque Creative, www.marquecreative.com

London lingerie Lascivious is as known for its beautifully designed and hand-stitched pieces as it is for its insouciant raunchiness – a steamy affair seemingly apt only for femmes fatales and sex sirens. However, its identity and marketing program unveils a playful, sweet and creative side: ribbons, heart-shaped boxes of bonbons and erotic play cards featuring today's top illustrators.

23 Monmouth Street
Covent Gardens
London WC2H 9DD
United Kingdom
www.coco-de-mer.co.uk
www.lascivious.co.uk

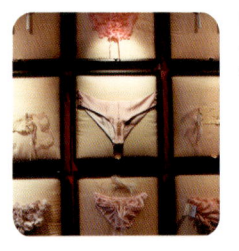

Lascivious by Chloe Hambien is an independent company sold online and at Coco de Mer.

165

Dark yet dazzling with sweetness, Lascivious's goal is to charm and tempt the customer.

167

Content

IY A Studio, www.iyastudio.co.uk

The UK's first luxury boutique with a conscience, Content brings a carefully selected collection of the world's best organic and natural beauty brands under one eco-elegant roof. IY A was commissioned to develop a complete brand communication and retail strategy that positioned the concept in the high-end beauty and skincare market while still retaining the ethical values of a brand that cares.

14 Bulstrode Street
Marylebone
London W1U 2JG
United Kingdom
www.beingcontent.com

Unnecessary chemicals are edited from the selection of products, and carrier bags are recyclable.

169

Communication materials use vegetable ink and have no special coatings that limit recycling options.

171

Hand-drawn illustrations of plants combine with reference pictures in homage to natural ingredients.

173

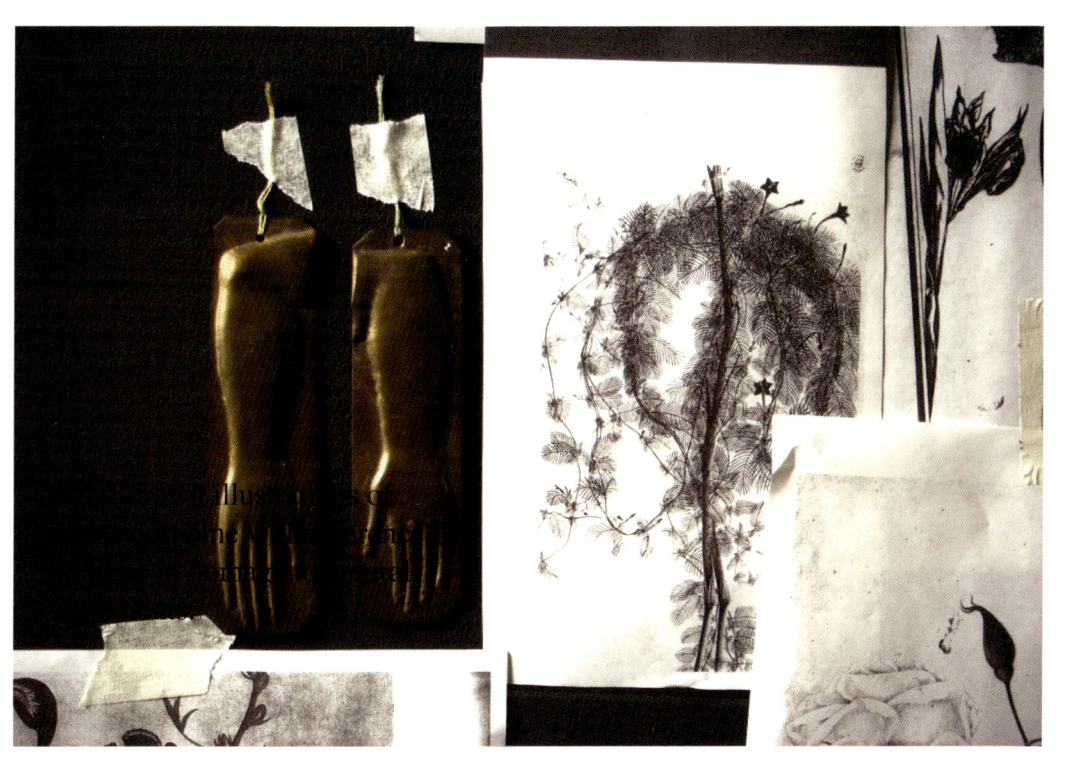

Sustainable materials and second-hand objects were incorporated throughout the store.

CONTENT
BEAUTY/WELLBEING

HOURS
Monday   closed
Tues-Sat 10.30 - 6.00
Sunday   12.00 - 5.00

Online
www.beingcontent.com

Women'Secret

Cla-se, www.cla-se.com

After years of providing the women of Spain with comfortable underwear and the coziest pajamas, Women'Secret has been firmly established in the collective mind as the place to go for intimates and furry slippers. Cla-se took over the store's branding and updated it with an online blog, innovative catalog layouts and a special line of packaging and in-store displays for the Basics collection.

Puerta Ferrisa, 7-9
08002 Barcelona
Spain
www.womensecret.com

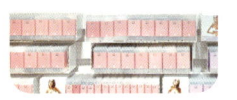

A children's line, maternity wear and a saucier line are all available in the Women'Secret catalog.

13 espalda libre con aros

13

17+75

17 costas multidecotes • 75 brasileiras

178

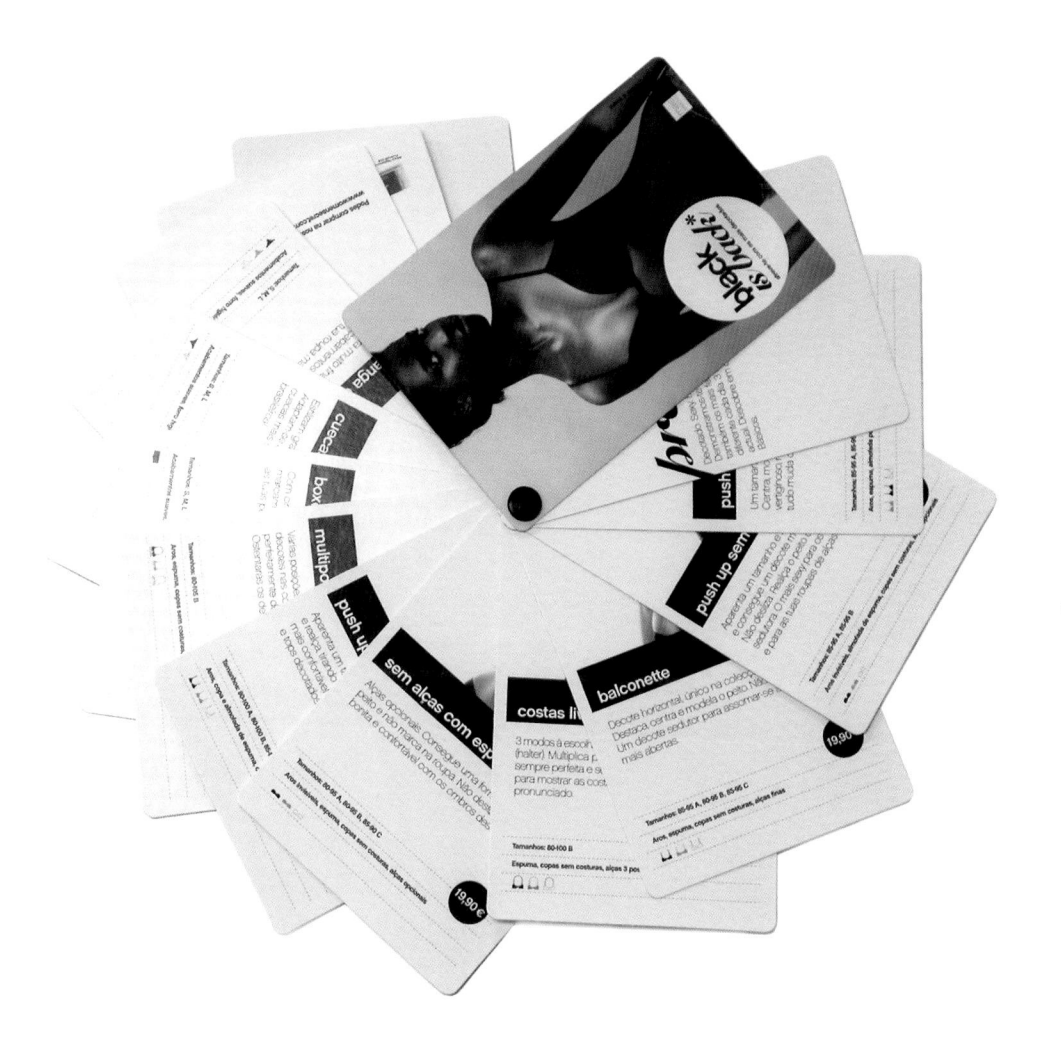

Product guides and packaging photos provide useful tips on finding the perfect fit.

The color-coded display for the Basics collection helps buyers to quickly pinpoint their items.

181

Fabrications

Jawa and Midwich, www.jawa-midwich.com

Barley Massey, the owner of Fabrications shop in London, had seen the work of Jawa and Midwich in conjunction with furniture designer Ryan Frank at the 100% East Expo. She commissioned Frank to design and build a counter top for the new shop and enlisted Jawa and Midwich to design a pattern and identity for Fabrications and to extend its use for the counter, shop front and stationery items.

fabrications
gallery / shop / studio

7 Broadway Market
Hackney
London E8 4PH
United Kingdom
www.fabrications1.co.uk

The logo hints at the store's goods: local, handmade products and knitting and sewing supplies.

contact

fabrications
7 broadway market,
hackney, london e8 4ph

+44 (0) 20 7275 8043
barley@fabrications1.co.uk
www.fabrications1.co.uk

fabrications

gallery / shop / studio

fabrications

welcome

we hope you enjoy all that 'fabrications' has to offer:

- unique handcrafted products and homewares locally sourced and eco-friendly

- hackney gifts and cards by hackney's artists and designers

- 'the hagedashery' – knitting and sewing supplies

we also offer a commissioning service and make items to order. please look through our portfolios, speak with the staff or visit www.fabrications1.co.uk for further information.

our aim is to inspire, enhance and demonstrate art and design's potential for positive, social and environmental change.

thank you for your custom.

please call by again!

185

The modular pattern branding can be extended indefinitely across the counter and store interior.

Bla Bla Bra

Tommy Li Design, www.tommylidesign.com

When Tommy Li Design was asked to develop a concept, store philosophy and brand identity for a colorful new brand of lingerie aimed at teenage girls, The Bla Bla Bra Citizens were born! These mischievous little characters each possess a unique personality and roam as they please all over the Bla Bla Bra identity, advertising tailor-made underwear with oodles of character to new age ladies.

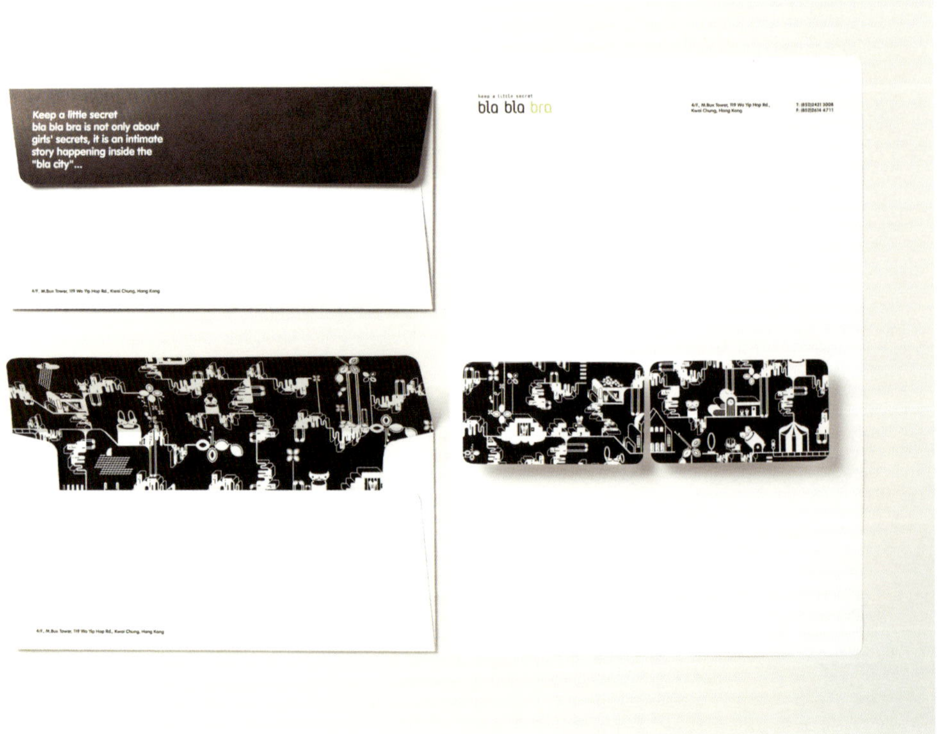

Shop B
39 Granville Road
Tsim Sha Tsui, Hong Kong
China
www.blablabra.com

Fun promotional items for the different Bla Citizens can be bought along with the clothes.

keep a little secret
bla bla bra

188

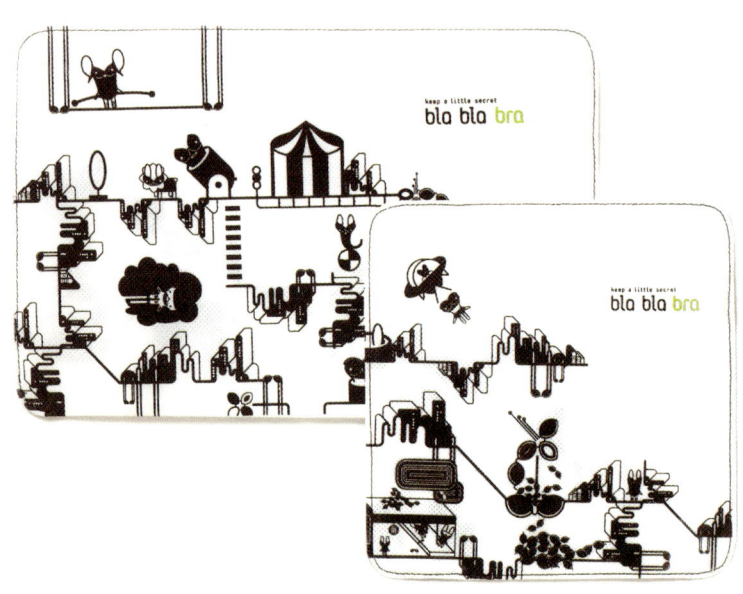

Bla Bla Bra's duotone identity breaks from classic black and white by inverting patterns and graphics.

190

The brand runs design contests and invites international talent to produce unique designer products.

191

192

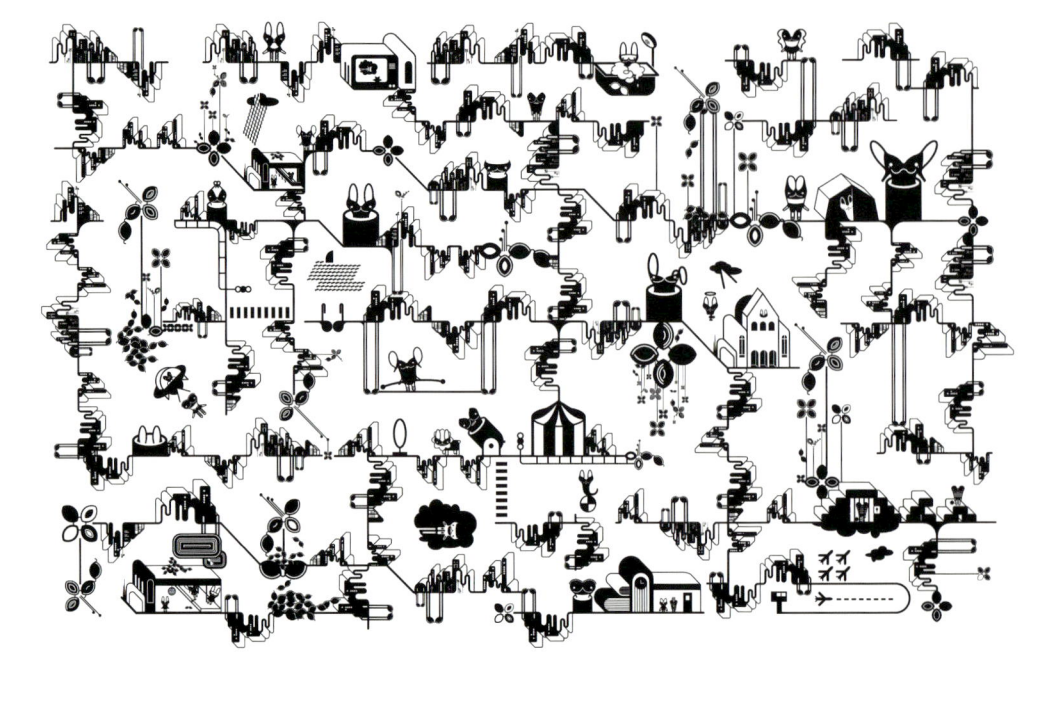

Interior graphics hint at the kind of shenanigans that Bla Citizens get up to in Bla City.

Tabooboo

BB/Saunders, www.bbsaunders.com

How do you sell sex on the high street and keep it playful, pretty, and a bit naughty? Soho sex boutique Tabooboo requested the skills of BB/Saunders to satisfy their fantasy: creating a retail experience that sits between the fashionable and seedy sides of the neighborhood. The result was a mythical forbidden garden, full of frilly knickers, to beguile shoppers into parting with their money.

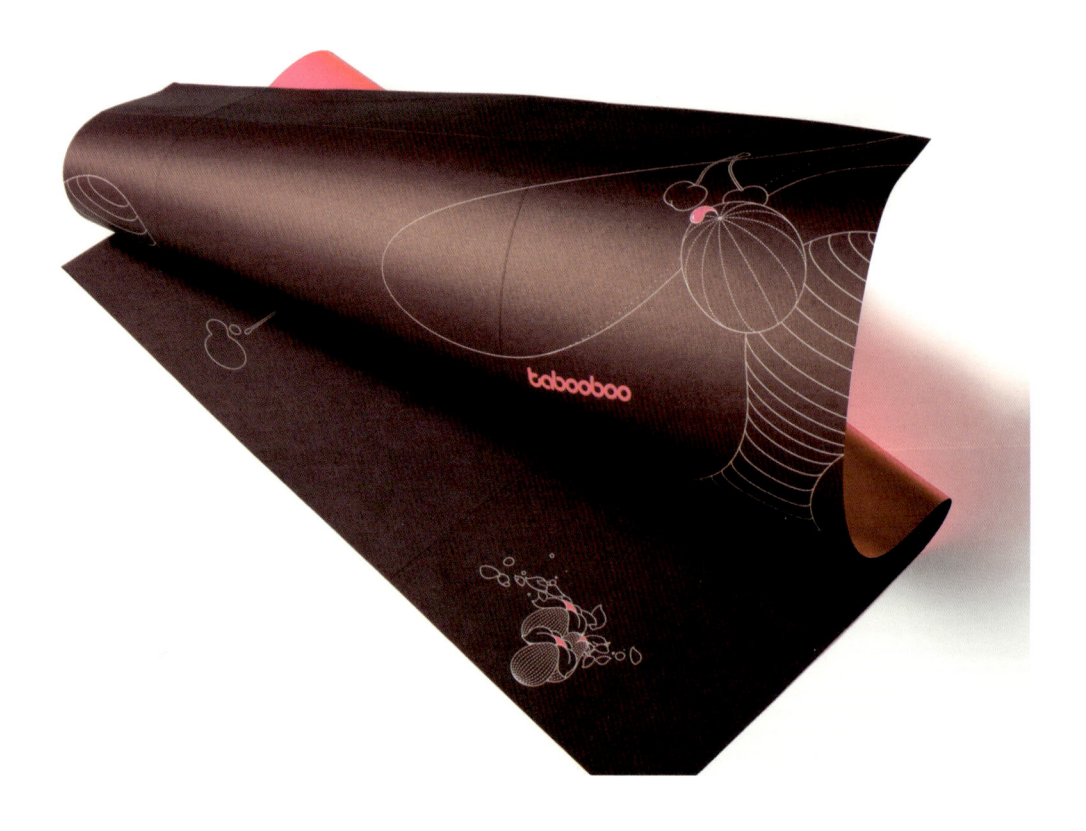

12 Foubert's Place
London W1F 7BH
United Kingdom
www.tabooboo.com

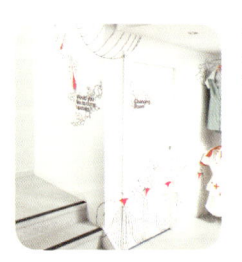

Creative vinyl graphics and embellishments help to make the most of the space on a small budget.

Opening Times
Monday   10am–7pm
Tuesday   10am–7pm
Wednesday   10am–7pm
Thursday   10am–8pm
Friday   10am–7pm
Saturday   10am–7pm
Sunday   12pm–6pm

195

My arm, your leg, your lips
An octopus times two
Twisted deep, no beginning, no end
We slide into another shape

Changing Rooms

Soft circle
to imaginary O
you find infinity,
thought wanders,
the ground departs
and weightless
state begins...

An illustrated graphic language of unspoken pleasures is combined with abstract erotic poetry.

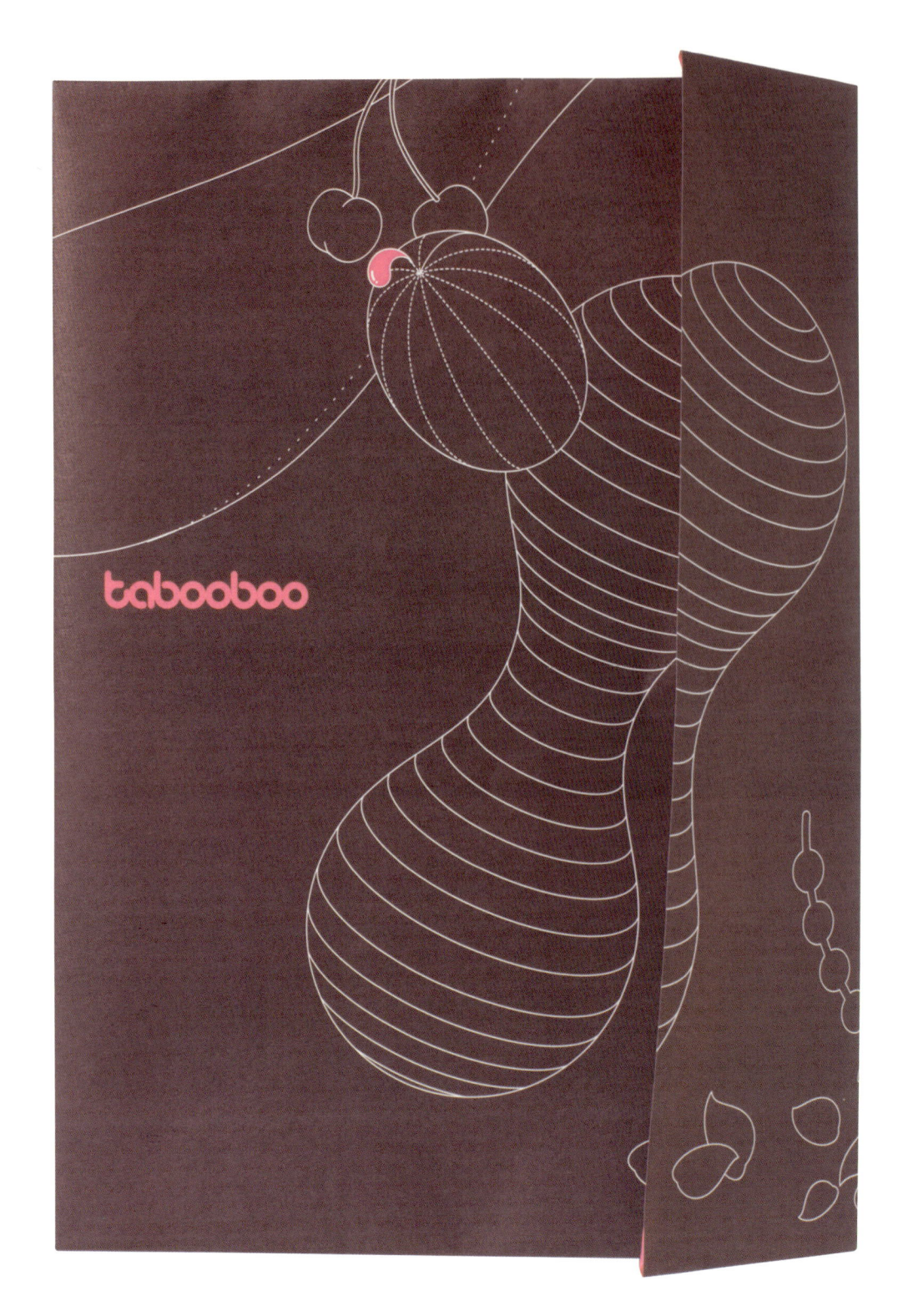

tabooboo

www.
tabooboo
.com
Unit 10
Grand Union Centre
West Row
Ladbroke Grove
London
W10 5AS

A discreet burgundy unfolds into a splash of tantalizing hot pink on one of the store's leaflets.

Prosays'

Tommy Li Design, www.tommylidesign.com

A Japanese cosmetic brand, Prosays' speaks to those who aspire to the highest quality of professional skincare and makeup. Tommy Li Design was asked to develop the new identity, from naming to packaging for multiple makeup and skincare products. A series of high-contrast, black-and-white photos featuring organic textures, insects and plants was developed as the main visual identity.

Counter at Harvey Nichol's
The Landmark
15 Queen's Road Central
Central, Hong Kong
China
www.prosays.com

Prosays' was founded by a team of professional cosmetic experts, hence its name.

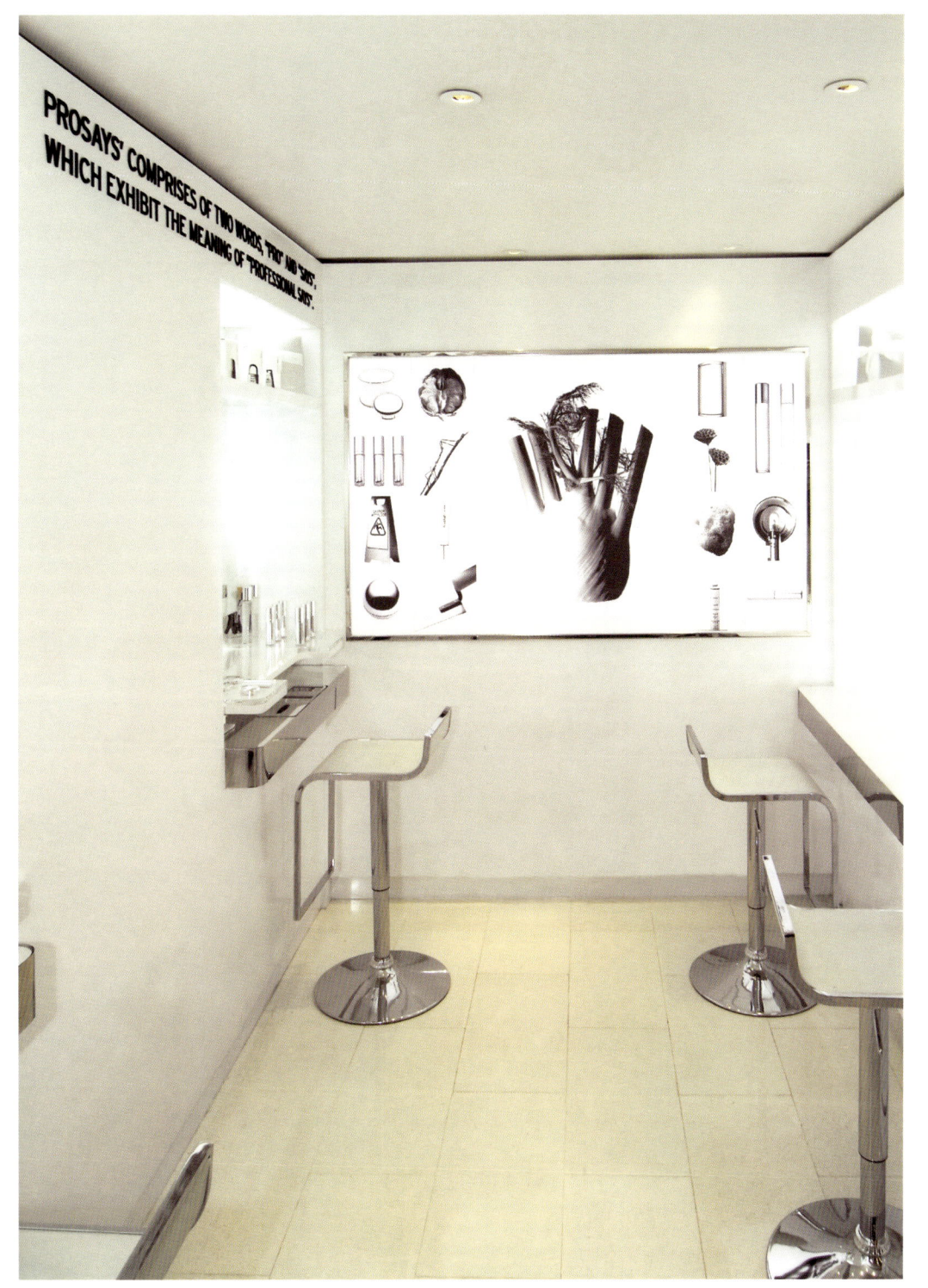

'PROSAYS' COMPRISES OF TWO WORDS, 'PRO' AND 'SAYS', WHICH EXHIBIT THE MEANING OF 'PROFESSIONAL SAYS'.

202

The beautiful close-ups of unusual animals and plants aim to perceive a new angle of beauty.

203

204

Sleek chrome interiors and products give the products an air of chic advanced technology.

Supersizing

Large sized multi-brand shops, often spreading over various floors, have a tricky task at hand: making sure that their identity is not completely diluted within the abundant space and array of merchandise. A strong logo and seasonal ad campaigns are staples, but the more astute also opt to cultivate a versatile personality to keep their customers surprised rather than conforming to the big enterprise standard. Instead of the routine pictograms, color-coded labels and custom elements permeate the interior design to help guide buyers along by intuition, while the store identity is gently emphasized by many subtle logo applications.

PUB

Bas Brand Identity, www.basbrandidentity.se

One of Stockholm's oldest department stores, first opened in 1882, PUB needed a new, modern orientation. Bas Brand Identity drew inspiration from the world of fashion blogs to translate their on-the-pulse read into a live and physical experience. Personality, interactivity and ongoing change are key – each floor has a different logo and identity that reflects the character of its contents.

Hötorget 13
Stockholm 111 57
Sweden
www.pub.se

Installations are set up on the different floors to stage the clothes in dynamic and appealing ways.

209

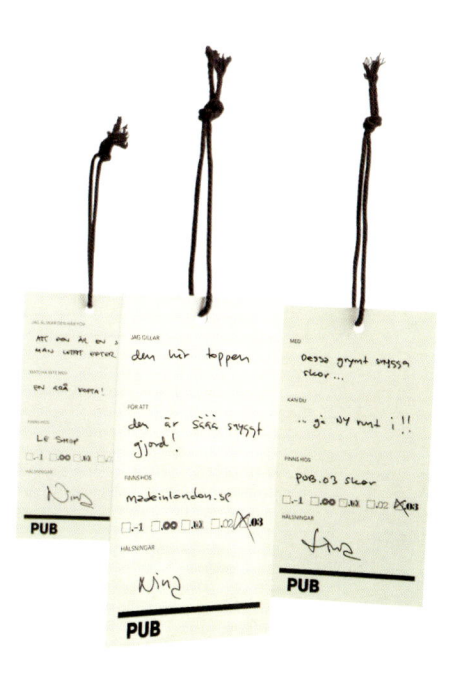

210

Floor 02 has a black and white lounge identity, while Floor 03 has an experimental fashion and art feel.

WANTS, NEEDS AND DESIRES AT PUB

I NEED

FOR CHRISTMAS

I WANT

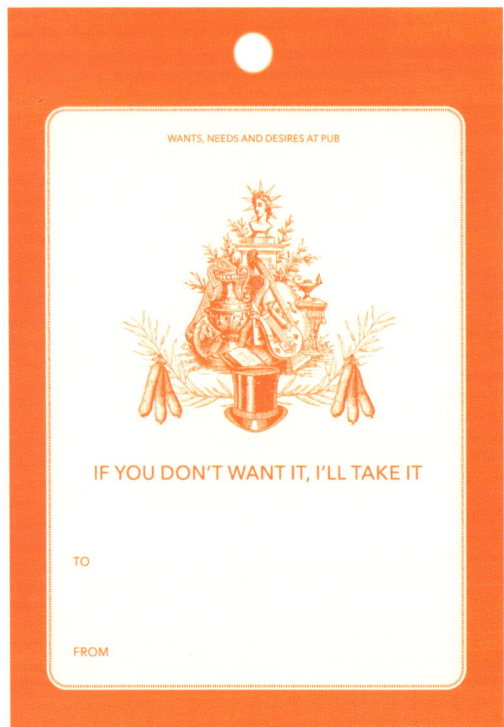

WANTS, NEEDS AND DESIRES AT PUB

IF YOU DON'T WANT IT, I'LL TAKE IT

TO

FROM

WANTS, NEEDS AND DESIRES AT PUB

THIS IS ALL YOU NEED

TO

FROM

WISHFUL THINKING

WANTS, NEEDS AND DESIRES AT PUB

SURE, THE HOLIDAYS ARE ALL ABOUT JOY, SWEET WARM WINE AND FINDING THE RIGHT NEW YEAR'S PARTY. BUT MOST OF ALL THIS IS THE SEASON FOR WISHING. WE'VE DONE A LITTLE EXPERIMENT AND DISCOVERED THAT WE GENERALLY HAVE THREE KINDS OF WISHES:

STUFF WE **NEED**, STUFF WE **WANT**, AND STUFF WE **DESIRE**.

EVERY CATEGORY ENCOMPASSES AMAZING STUFF, AND TO GUIDE YOU WE'VE MADE OUR OWN DEFINITION OF THEM AND WHAT YOU CAN WISH FOR THIS CHRISTMAS. **HAPPY HOLIDAYS!**

PUB ORDINARIE ÖPPETTIDER: VARDAGAR 10–19, LÖR 10–17, SÖN 11–17.
10 DEC – 23 DECEMBER: ALLA DAGAR 10–20, JULAFTON 10–14,
ANNANDAGEN 10–17, NYÅRSAFTON 10–14. **WWW.PUB.SE**

213

The Christmas campaign tags and cards organize the consumer goods into wants, needs and desires.

214

All of PUB's carrier bags are environmentally friendly, and can be customized with tags and stickers.

FASHIO NISTAS ANONY MOUS

THE *2007* ANNUAL CONVENTION WILL BE HELD AT
PUB.03 SEPTEMBER 27

HONOURABLE GUESTS: VIVIENNE WESTWOOD, MINIMARKET, SURFACE 2 AIR, APRIL 77 MARC JACOBS, TOM FORD SUNGLASSES, A*N*D, PAUL & JOE BEAUTÉ, NICE COLLECTIVE JU$T ANOTHER RICH KID, LOUIS DE GAMA, KAVIAR GAUCHE, TROVATA, FORTE FORTE ETC..

FASHIONISTAS ANONYMOUS SWEDEN

WELCOME!

SEPTEMBER 2007   THIS IS A MESSAGE FROM PUB.
THANKS FOR CARRYING IT AROUND TOWN.   WWW.PUB.SE

Parad

Design Bureau Proekt, www.proekt.co.uk

The interior for the new Parad boutique — a chain of classic shopping emporiums in Moscow — was given an unconventional treatment by Design Bureau Proekt as part of a general re-branding. While carrier bags are inspired by popular movies like *Pirates of the Caribbean* and *A Clockwork Orange,* the interior wall graphics and huge mirrors seem to allude to a warped version of *Alice in Wonderland.*

Kutuzovsky prospekt, 14
121165 Moscow
Russia
www.parad-shoes.ru

Light-emitting diodes with changing colors highlight the shelves and drawers in the store.

217

The Fall/Winter 08 catalog featured postcards of designer goods floating in space, packed in space-age bags.

219

220

After the space issue, the Spring/Summer catalogue was designed as a candy-colored glossy fashion magazine.

Caban

Blok Design, www.blokdesign.com

In developing the identity for Caban, Blok Design needed to provide a visual sense of what the brand stood for and differentiate it from a highly cluttered marketplace. The identity needed to be memorable: classic yet undeniably chic. The Caban wordmark is simple, honest and fresh. It also creates its unique sense of space by its corner positioning, expressing the dynamic spirit of the brand.

2912 Granville Street
Vancouver, BC V6H 3J7
Canada
www.caban.com

Like the identity, the Caban space was designed to be approachable: it is both open and intimate.

223

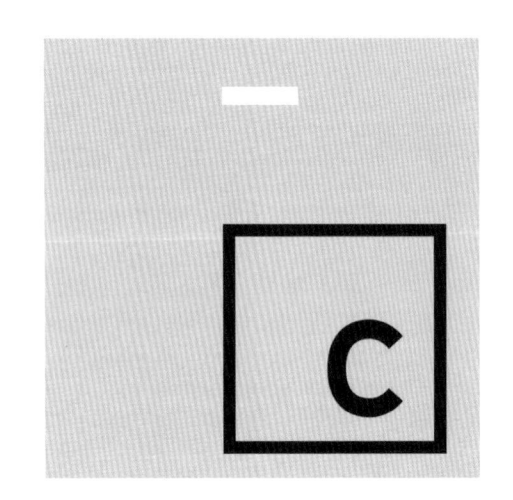

The chocolate and blue color palette and bold typography are a consistent thread throughout the system.

225

Fena

Beetroot Design Group, www.beetroot.gr

One of the largest multi-stores in Greece, the Fena store in Thessaloniki spans four floors stocked with popular brands for men, women and children. To tackle this giant's visual communication, the multi-faceted Beetroot Design Group used two kinds of elements: a core identity based on images of leaves and a themed seasonal campaign that breathes in new illustrations and patterns.

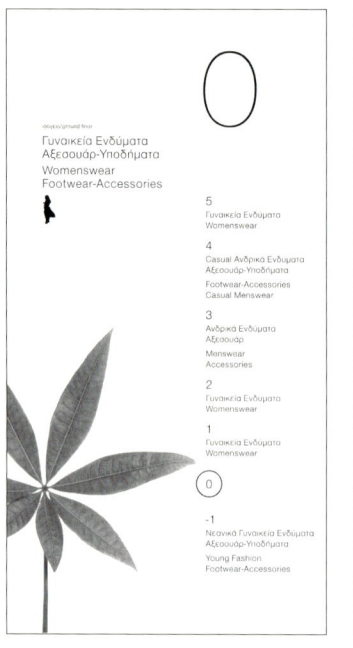

14 Dimokritou Street
Finikas
55134 Thessaloniki
Greece
www.fena.gr

Kaleidoscopic images from the seasonal campaign adorn light boxes as part of the indoor decoration.

fena.

SPRING SUMMER 2006
**IMAGINE
MORE**

228

The leaf graphics are applied to bags, labels and signage, while the campaigns change every six months.

230

The Spring/Summer 08 campaign features dream-like animals, insects and elegant characters.

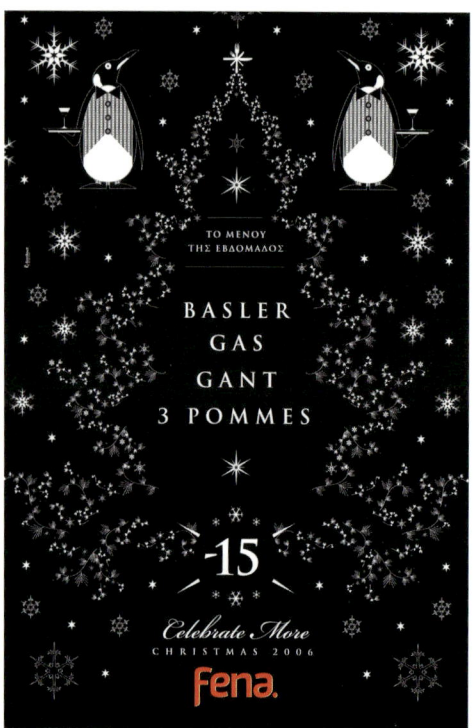

The graphics for Fall/Winter 07 are structured line drawings which are easy to integrate to patterns.

233

Naked

FOUR IV, www.fouriv.com

Leading graphic and interior design agency FOUR IV created a completely new retail experience for Turkey's fashion conscious consumer group. Naked is Istanbul's first multi-brand store, where black dominates across two mezzanines of high-gloss resin floors, black polished walls and theatrical spotlighting, within a sculptural display of copper and stainless steel rods shooting out of the ceiling.

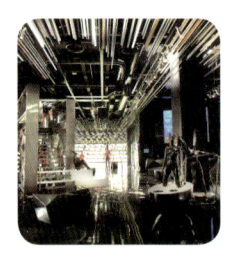

Istinye Bayiri Caddesi
Istanbul 34460
Turkey
www.naked.com.tr

Dynamic forms and 3D patterns combine with striking details to create movement and intrigue.

235

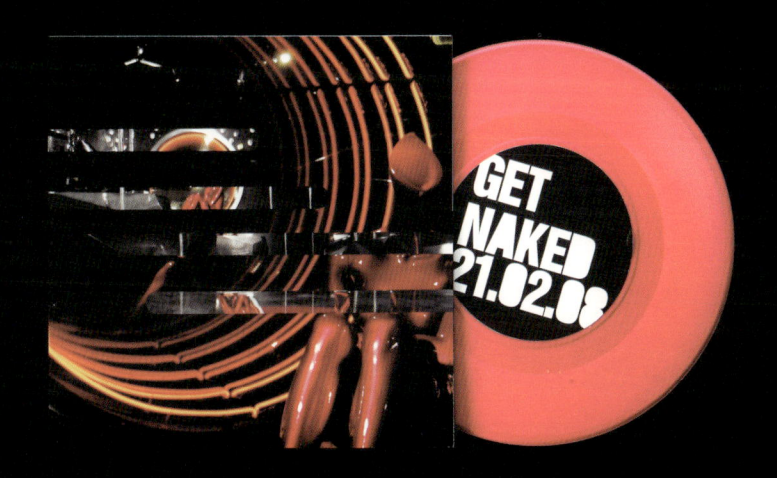

The controversial name and covetable packaging was created to appeal to a brand-savvy audience.

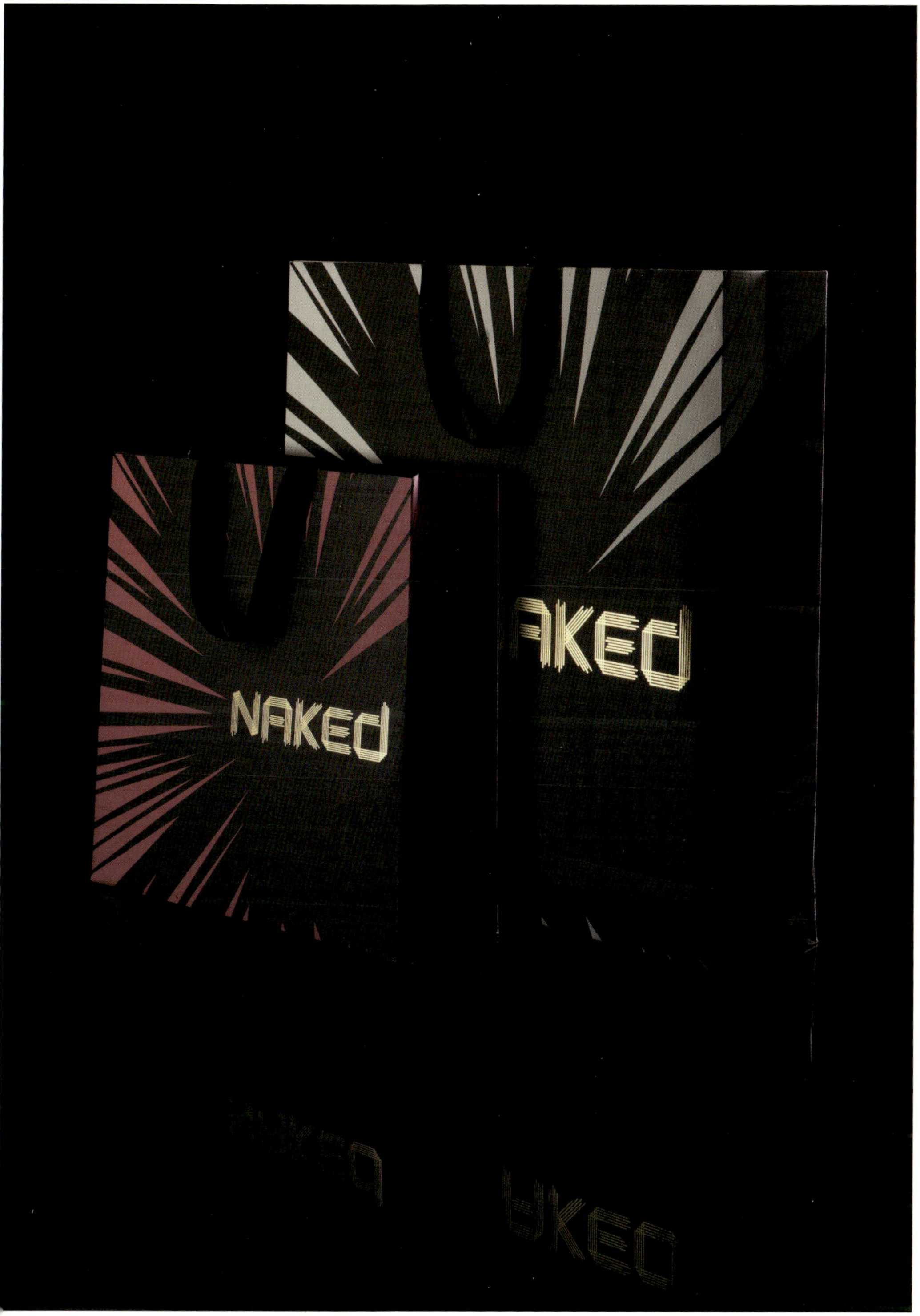
NAKED
NAKED

238

The branding is integrated with the architecture – the identity's letters are formed from the rod system.

Inspiration

Bas Brand Identity, www.basbrandidentity.se

The "living and giving" concept is about combining an offer of products which are exclusive and of high quality, while still managing to be seasonal, more accessible, and with a quick turnaround. This concept was conceived by Bas Brand Identity for the Inspiration store, along with a full graphic identity, in-store communication and packaging featuring a growing, living, plant-like pattern.

Storgatan 44
Ängelholm 262 32
Sweden
www.inspirationsbutiken.se

The store's aim is to always inspire customers to find something great to give as a gift or bring home for themselves.

Välj rätt redskap!

Cicileringsjärn
Formar dekorationer av citrusfrukter och används som rivjärn.

Äppelurkärnare
Gör att du snabbt och smidigt tar ut kärnhuset ur äpplen.

Ballongvisp express
Innehåller en kula för att snabbare vispa t ex grädde eller få en jämnare smet.

Kuljärn
Gör fina kulor av frukter och grönsaker.

Stekpincett
Gör det enkelt att vända mat vid stekning och grillning. Undvik att sticka i stekytan med t ex en gaffel eftersom köttsaften kan rinna ut.

Kniv – hårda ostar

Kniv – parmesanost

Kniv – mjuka ostar

242

Plock & Redskap

Cheese slicers and teapots are some of the kitchen objects that display the plant-like pattern.

Marui

Drill Inc., www.drill-inc.jp

Marui department store had been known for its inexpensive merchandise for college students. However, wishing to expand its customer base to a more urban, lifestyle-inspired clientele, Marui opened a new store in Yurakucho, an area renowned for its cluster of luxury department stores, and recruited Drill Inc. to reintroduce it as a quality-conscious urban store in an area where elegance is the norm.

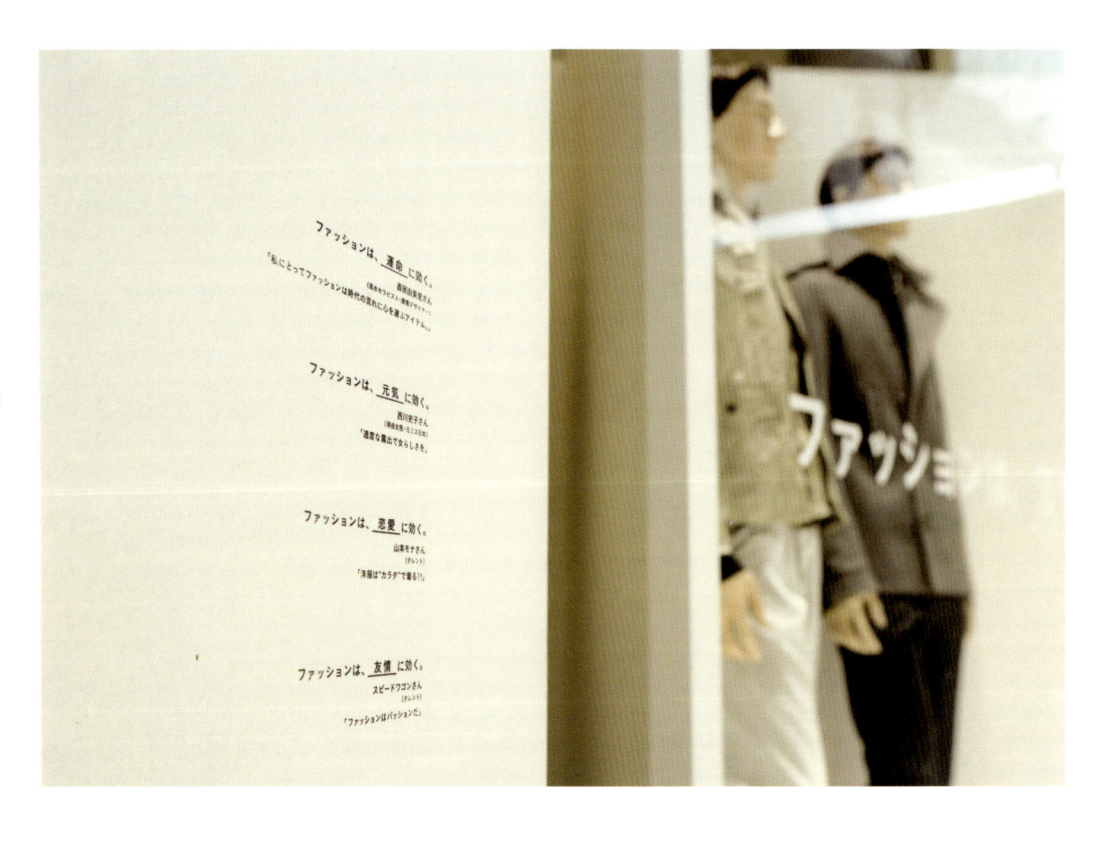

2-7 Yurakucho, Chiyoda-ku
Tokyo 100-0006
Japan
www.0101.co.jp

Marui's international shopping website, maruione.jp, also offers information on Japanese street fashion and culture.

215

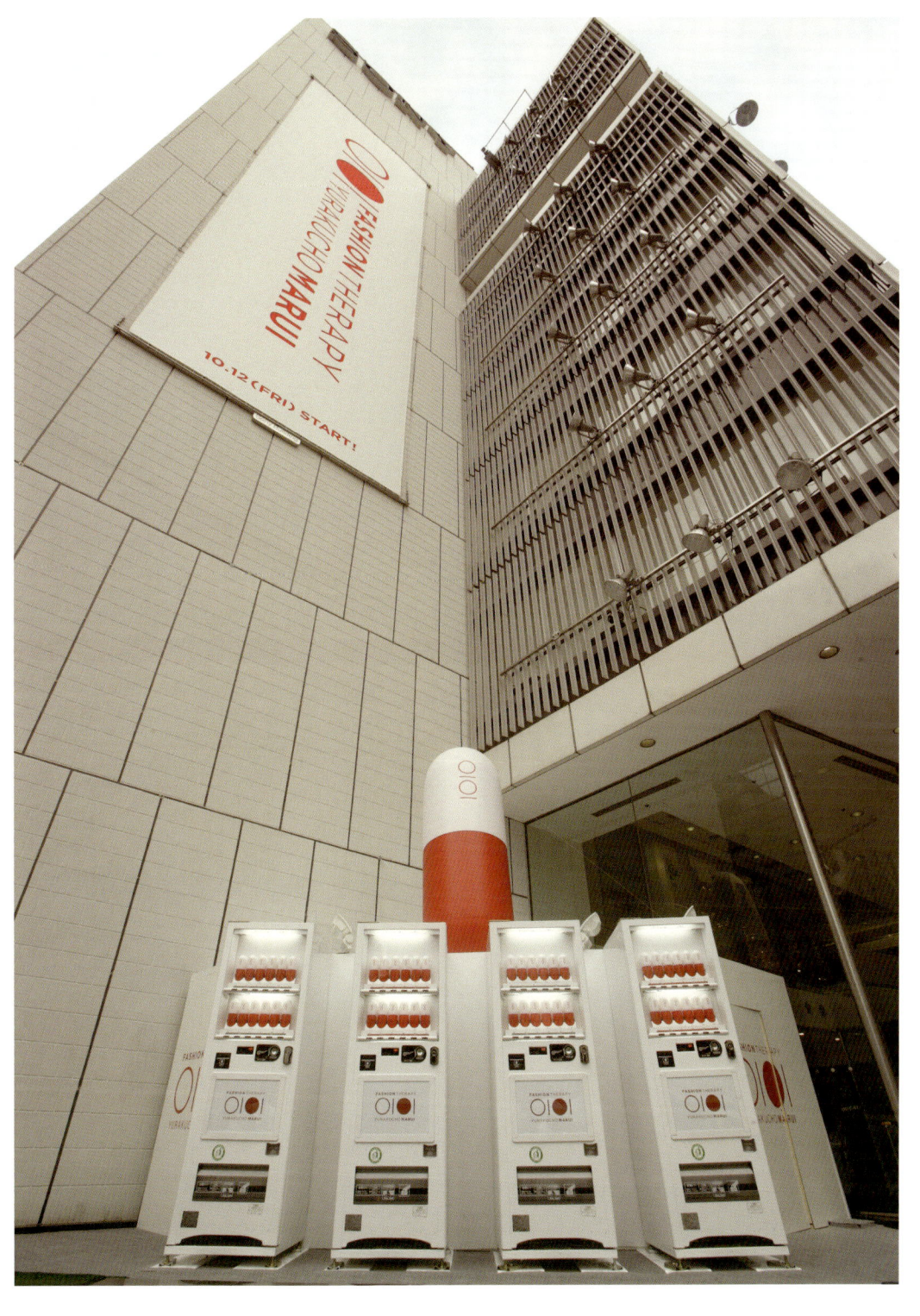

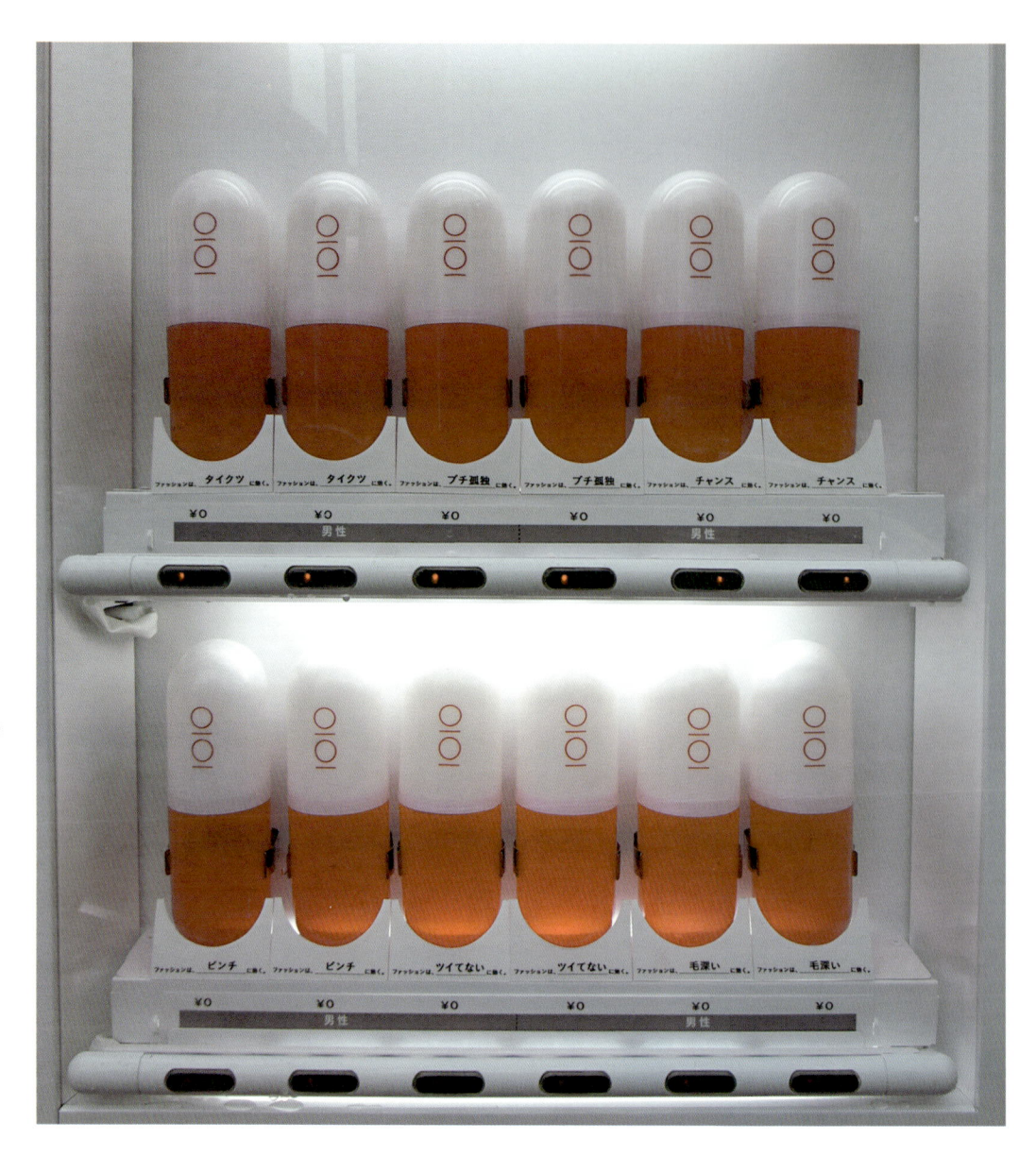

The "fashion therapy" concept urges urbanites to seek fashion as a way of comforting their feelings.

217

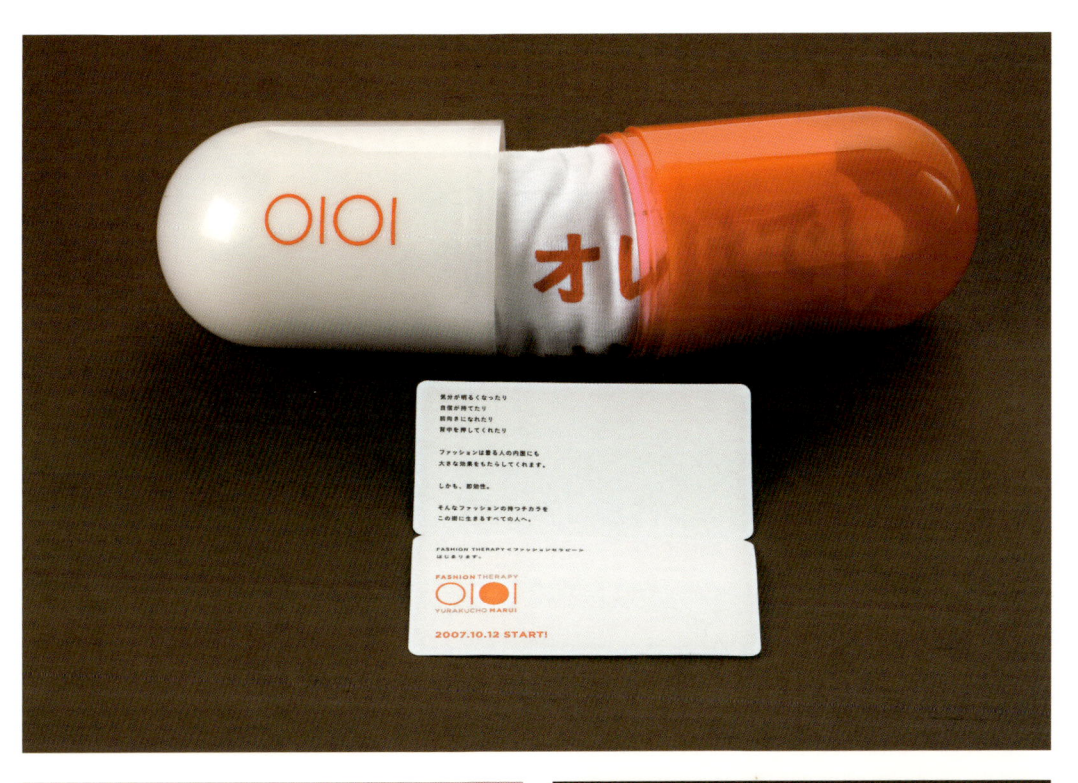

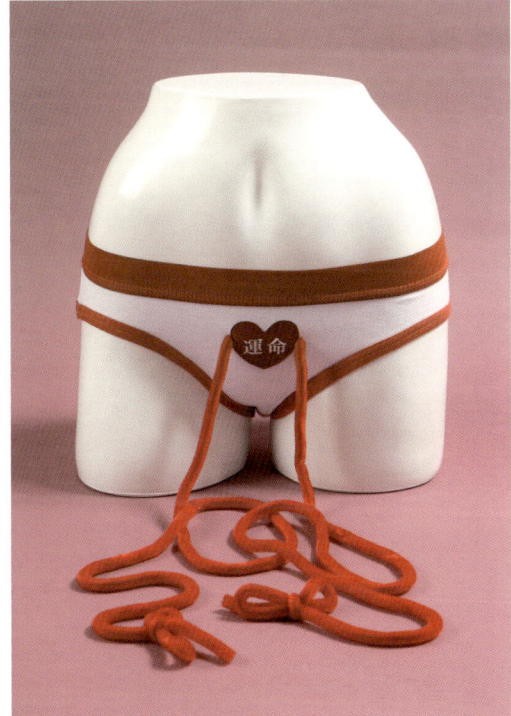

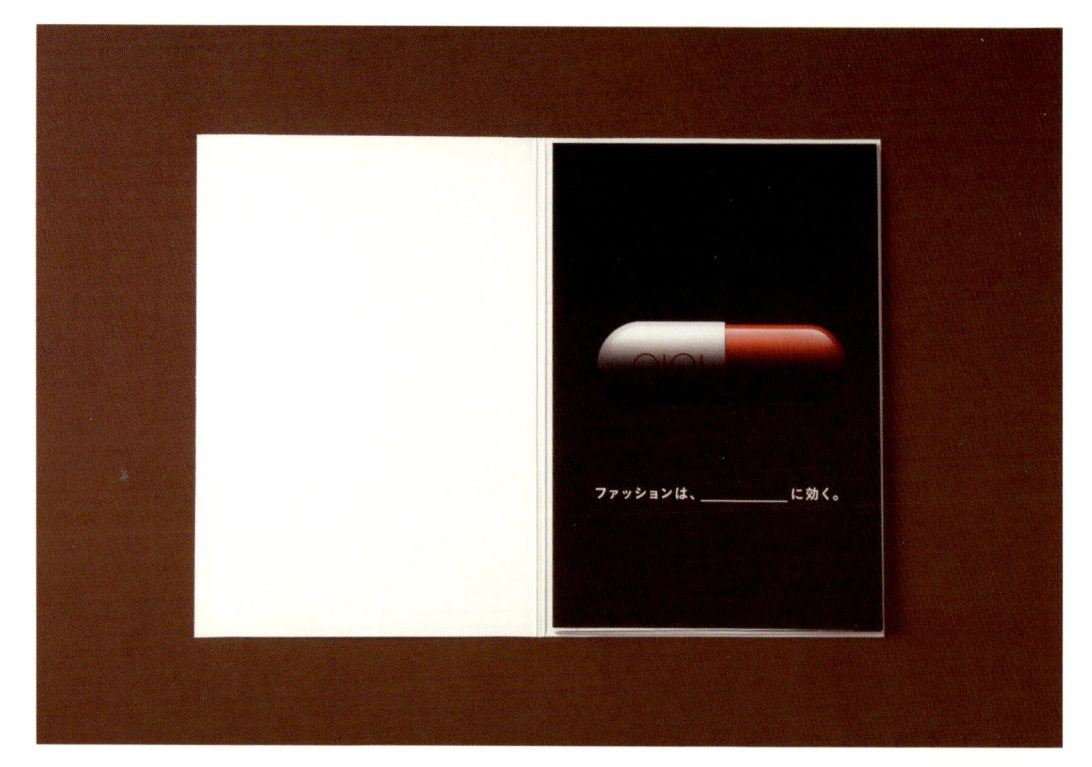

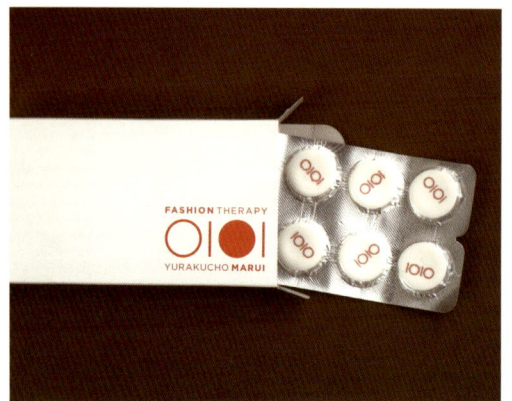

The capsule icon indicates the prescription aspect, and print identity acquires a "clinical" look.

249

有楽町からハッピーに。

10.12 (FRI) START! | FASHION THERAPY YURAKUCHO MARUI

おしゃれをしないとカラダに毒です。

FASHION THERAPY YURAKUCHO MARUI

おしゃれをしないとカラダに毒です。

FASHION THERAPY YURAKUCHO MARUI

251

The red circle in the icon is echoed throughout the print ads in the form of balloons and rings.

Creed
& Concept

These are shops and brands whose identities are molded pre-eminently by their personal philosophies, beliefs and ideas. With themes ranging from social reinsertion to social dissidence, to poking fun of designer snobbery or defending tongue-in-cheek kitsch, it is hard to pinpoint a single aesthetic path. However, visual imagery based on abstractions often shines with a more definite and unitary notion, resulting in a unique, strong personality, and thus a solid identity. Parallel activities such as cultural and social events propel these stores further into the state-of-the-art realm and give rise to opportunities for extra promotional goods like magazines, household objects and shop t-shirts.

Bozar Shop
Base Design, www.basedesign.com

A bookstore in Brussels dedicated entirely to the arts, Base Design's first store was opened in collaboration with publisher Actar, architects Lhoas&Lhoas, and Bozar Shop itself – the Palais des Beaux-Arts. The identity and promotional items for this culture-packed superstore use no-fuss, fun snapshots of store workers and random people and friends, combined with light-hearted messages.

15, rue Ravenstein
1000 Brussels
Belgium
www.bozarshop.com

Bozar Shop also has a café and a children's section with books and games.

BO
ZAR
SHOP
**COLIN
BOUCHAT**

BO
ZAR
SHOP
**JACQUES
de NEUVILLE**

256

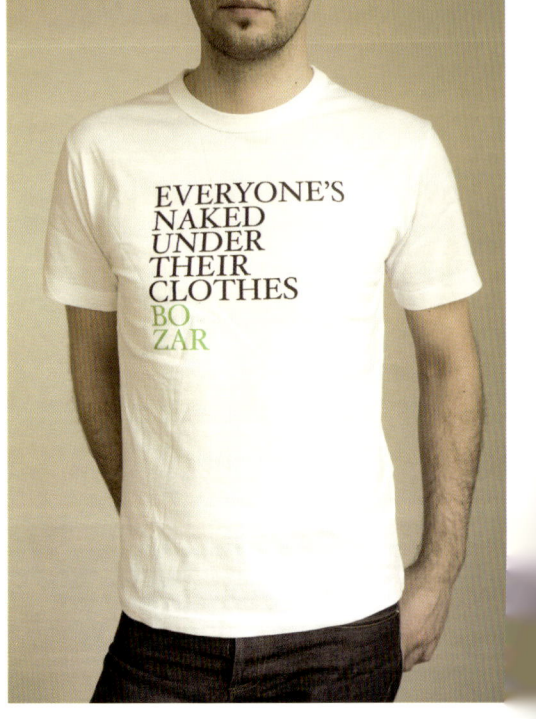

BO
ZAR
SHOP
IS
COMING

OPEN 7/7 - 10:00 > 22:00 - OPENING SOON

WHERE
IS MY
BO
ZAR
SHOP
?

257

Text is context-specific and varies according to the application or accompanying image.

Chapter 2

Mono, www.mono-1.com

A non-profit project of The Women's Alliance, Chapter 2 is a second-hand clothing store that helps reintroduce disadvantaged women into the work force. Everything from the name itself to design studio Mono's identity system, which uses recycled wallpaper scraps for store tags and business cards, was created to underscore the belief that everything – and everyone – deserves a second chance.

250 NW 9th Street
Miami, FL 33136
United States
www.chapter2clothing.org

Chapter 2 offers high-end second-hand clothing and items, as well as support and training.

259

260

The catalog shows different things that a $30 donation might buy to help decorate the store.

The stickers are used to alter custom or already-existing identity items, making each piece unique.

Men's ch.2 Women's

CLOTHING

A NEW STORE
A NEW CHAPTER

Introducing Chapter Two,
a unique, upscale clothing store in
The Dorsey House in Overtown that combines
great fashion with an even greater good.

A nonprofit project of the Women's Alliance,
Chapter Two uses the revenue from sales to
help provide professional attire and career skills
training to low-income women
seeking employment.

ch2clothing.org
250 NW Ninth Street
Miami, FL 33136
305-377-2755

Dissidence by Boris

lg2boutique, www.lg2boutique.com

Building on the Boris brand, lg2boutique launched a line of street wear for men and women called Dissidence by Boris. Maintaining Boris's edgy theme, the point of purchase creatively depicts a rebellious street scene with a protester waving a Boris flag. Urban guerrilla tactics like stenciling and cheap xeroxing are referenced throughout the posters, promo cards and a print campaign.

Available at Blank
4276 Saint-Laurent Blvd.
Montreal, H2X 2T7
Canada
www.biereboris.com

Hoodies, utilitarian jackets and other urban uniforms in suitably dark colors fill the racks.

265

266

The garments are manufactured in Montreal and sold in local boutiques called Blank.

Hitherto

Stuart White, www.stuartwhite.eu

With many aims in mind, Hitherto opened to offer an antidote to over-design, to make local art accessible, to shine light on the beauty of everyday objects, to relish in all things handmade and to find the unique in an over-saturated market. Local artist and designer Stuart White has graced the store's flyers, wrapping paper and general identity with his prolific illustrations and style.

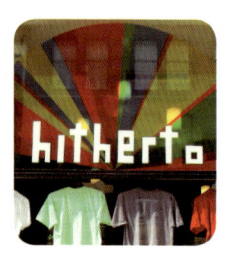

Hitherto at Tinderbox
McIntyre Hogg Building Unit 4
141 Ingram Street
Glasgow G1 1EJ1
United Kingdom
www.narratively.eu

Hitherto is a shop, gallery and performance space tucked in the back of the Tinderbox Café in Glasgow.

269

270

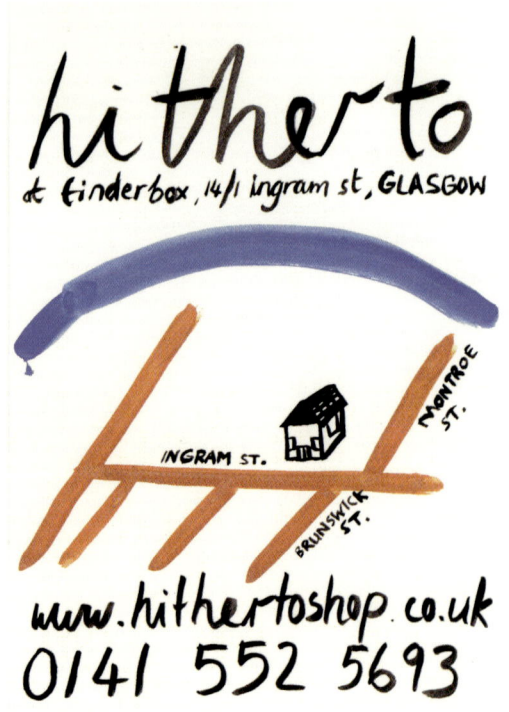

Unusual illustrations and original art are distinctive features that build up the store's character.

hitherto
AT TINDERBOX.
McINTYRE HOGG BUILDING.
14/1 INGRAM STREET,
GLASGOW G1 1EJ1
www.hithertoshop.co.uk
0141 552 5693

272

Illustrations for handmade wallets, LP sleeves and the store's own 7-inch single.

The logo gets the woven treatment and a 3D version; the website is invaded by handmade elements.

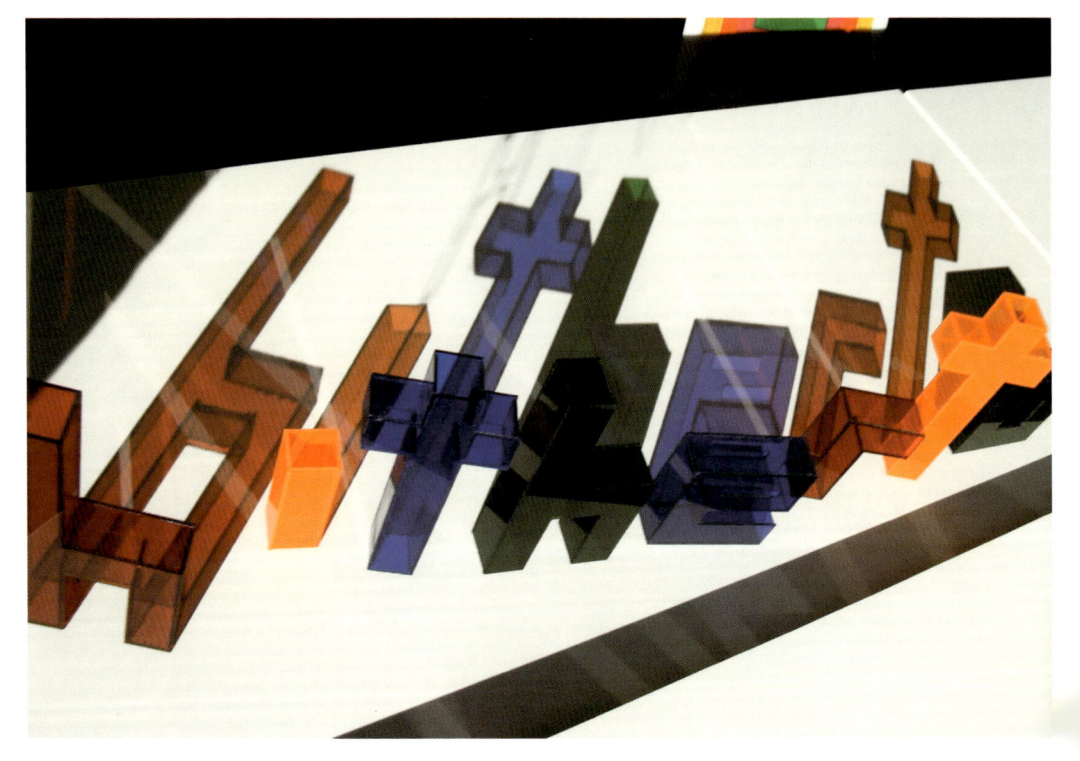

Hitherto Nose Handkercheif

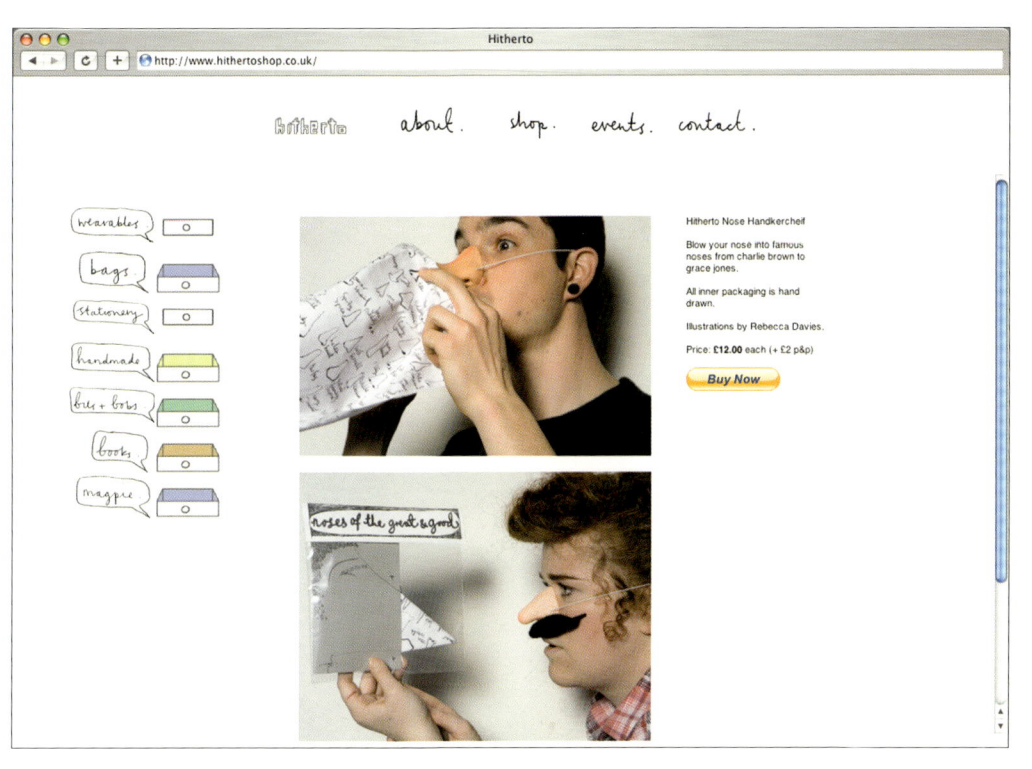

Blow your nose into famous noses from charlie brown to grace jones.

All inner packaging is hand drawn.

Illustrations by Rebecca Davies.

Price: **£12.00** each (+ £2 p&p)

Buy Now

Test Tube

Block Branding, www.blockbranding.com

Specializing in unique designer things, Test Tube makes ordinary objects extraordinary. Block Branding's identity and visual communication for the store mirrors its quirky nature, satirizing and celebrating consumer culture at the same time with deliberately ambiguous advertising. "periodic table" stickers have an obvious link to the store's name, but the *Space Invaders* window graphics are left open to interpretation.

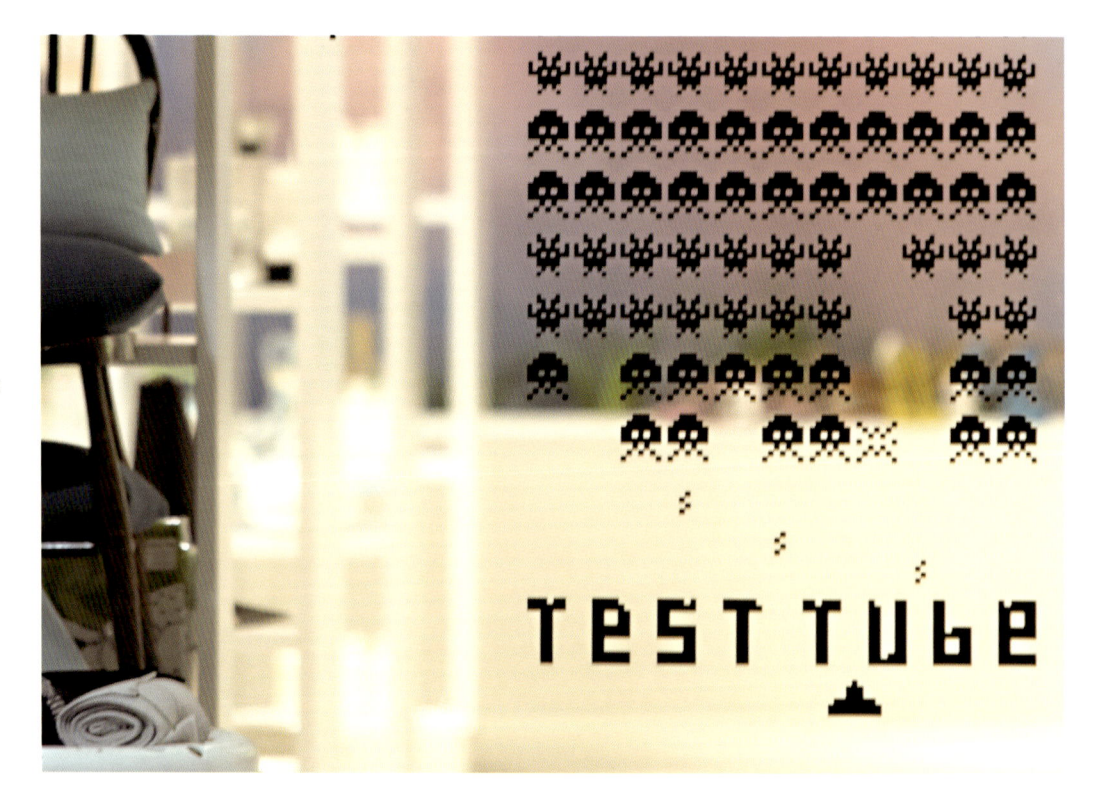

Shop 6
595 Beaufort Street
CNR Chelmsford Road
Mt. Lawley, WA 6050
Australia
www.testtubeobjects.com

Block aimed to create an atmosphere that didn't look mass-produced or homogeneous.

277

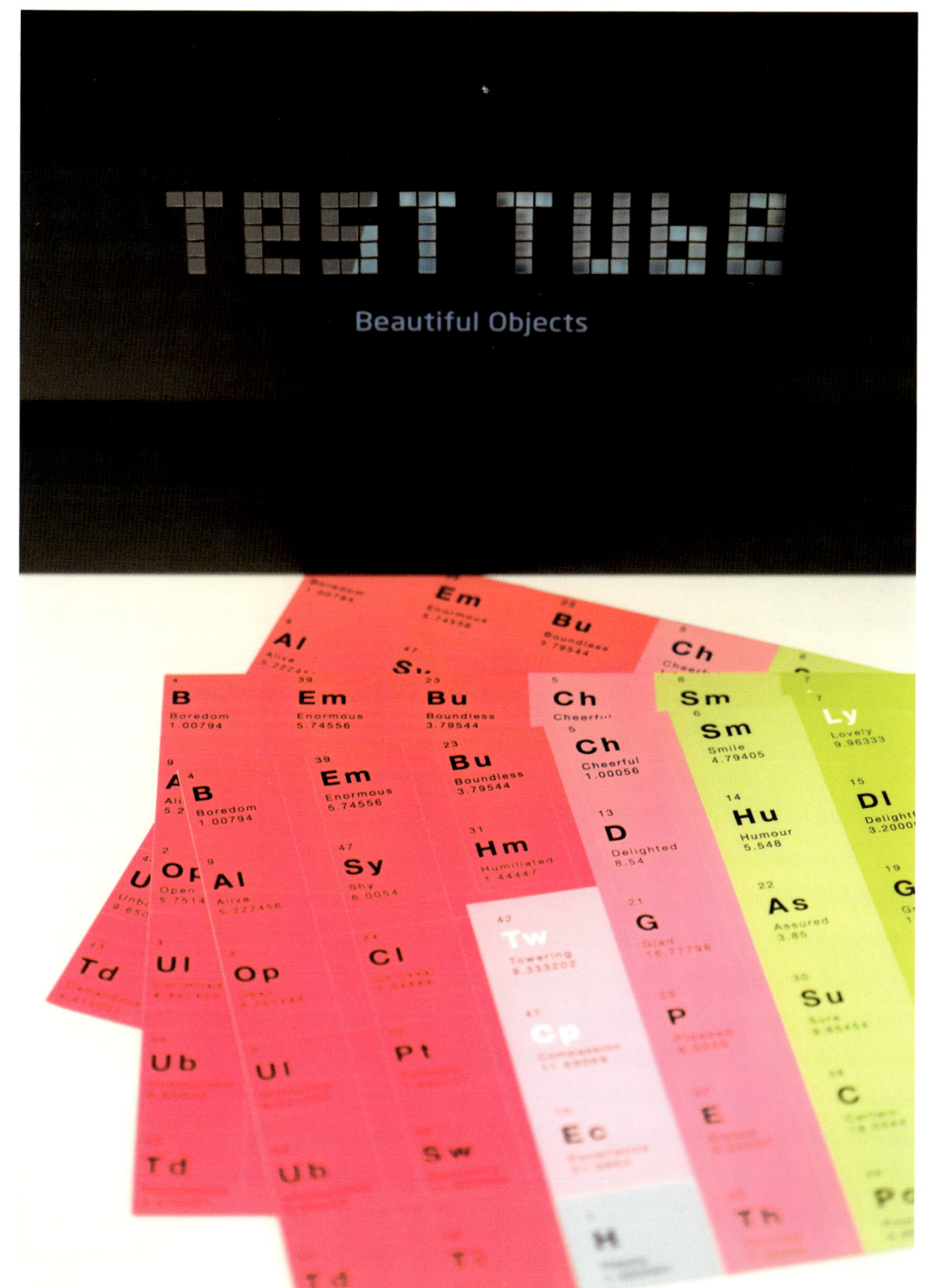

278

Lenticular business card and a quarterly advertising campaign in email-friendly PDF format.

TEST TUBE

Issue 03 2007

SPRING: LESS ORDINARY

EATING 'BOUT MY GENERATION

From ancient Greek terracotta wine jugs to the spork, mankind's history can be mapped by looking at the objects that fill our kitchen cabinets.

What, and how we eat has always been in a constant state of change. In the space of just forty years Australia has moved from a predominantly Anglo-centric food culture, through a period of southern-European influence, to a contemporary world of Asian-inspired fusion.

We have not only seen vast changes in what we eat but also how we eat. Once upon a time a pasta fork would have been alien technology to anyone outside an Italian home, and imagine the look you would have garnered a generation ago if you had suggested that guests at the 'average' Australian dinner party eat with chopsticks.

The evolving relationship we all have with food and how we consume it has always been fertile inspiration for designers.

It is inevitable that any designer of objects will, at some point, have to concern themselves with dining, food preparation or food storage. Every generation reinvents, rediscovers and reinterprets this world for their peers and they leave behind fascinating artifacts that will define each era for those that come after.

Pierpoint

Purpose, www.purpose.co.uk

London studio Purpose was asked to create a distinctive identity for Pierpoint, a hairdresser with its own brand of products located in the heart of Soho. The shop's location in what is known as London's red light district instigated Purpose to create a memorably cheeky brand identity. This identity was applied to all stationery, merchandise, interior graphics and the website.

11 Archer Street
London W1D 7AZ
United Kingdom
www.pierpointhairdressing.com

The uniforms are fitted with their own tongue-in-cheek slogans: "I'll Do You Next!"

281

282

Pierpoint Hairdressing in the heart of Soho

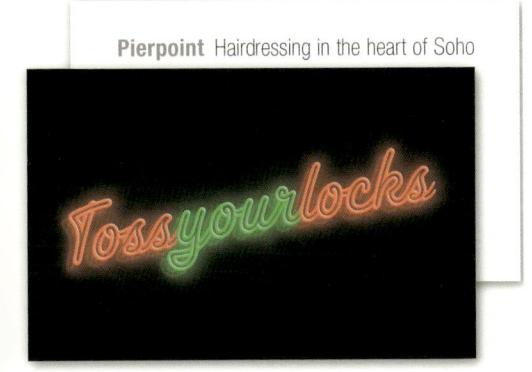

283

The neon lights of the sex industry are used to subvert otherwise innocent hairdressing phrases.

Skanno

Chris Bolton, www.chrisbolton.org

A one-of-a-kind concept store, Skanno in Helsinki houses product design, books, a full-fledged restaurant, a florist and an art gallery, as well as being host to different cultural events. Graphic designer Chris Bolton was commissioned to design the store's graphic identity as well as interior graphics — from wallpaper and restroom pictograms to product display counters and window stickers.

Skanno Salmisaarentalo
Porkkalankatu 13 G
001800 Helsinki
Finland
www.skanno.fi

Interior and furniture graphics were produced with the idea of metamorphosis and change.

285

286

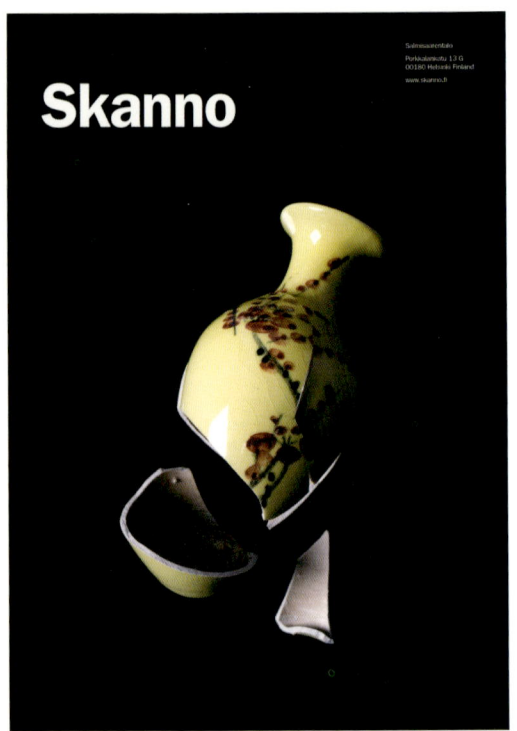

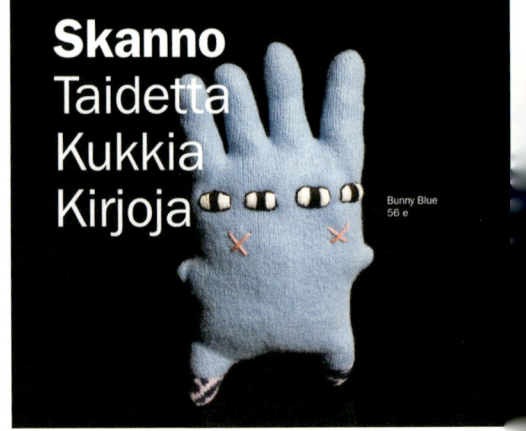

Posters conveying store concepts (here, "out with the old, in with the new") and store stationery.

Skanno

Salmisaarentalo
Porkkalankatu 13 G
FIN-00180 Helsinki Finland

288

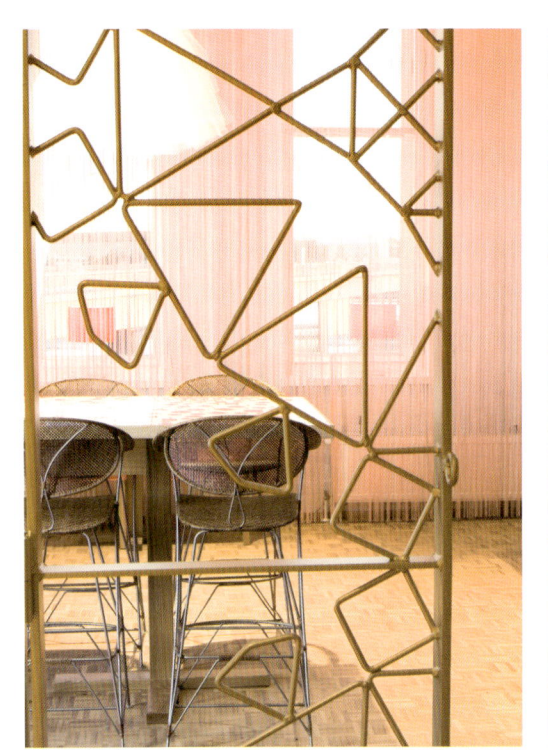

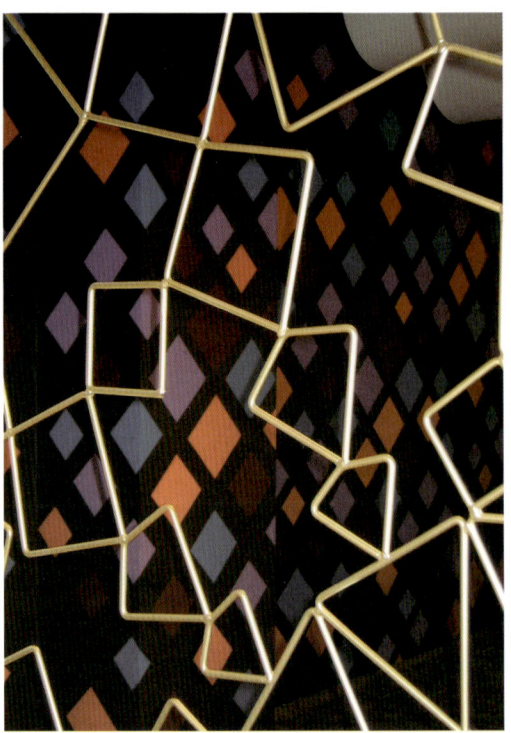

Geometric shapes and pictograms are used to link the different areas of the store and restaurant.

Wawas Barcelona Shop

7 potencias, www.7potencias.net

Far from the accustomed tourist trap, the Wawas Barcelona Shop revels in all things local and homemade with only a hint of good old designer kitsch. Highly saturated photos of some of the city's most improbable corners and most frightfully ordinary habits adorn shop postcards, mugs and product stands, creating a store identity that doesn't hide its feelings about the gloriously quotidian.

Carders, 14
08002 Barcelona
Spain
www.wawasbarcelona.com

Amongst alternative city guides and Catalan curiosities, one can find local designer gems.

291

TAPAS
PESCADITOS 7.00 CALAMARES 6.60
CHIPIRONES 6.60 CROQUETAS 5.60
GAMBAS PLANCHA 18.30 BRAVAS 4.40
SALADAS 8.00 ANCHOAS 5.40
SARDINAS 4,90 7.00
BOQUERONES 5.20 PULPITOS 8.00
MEJILLONES 6.40
BOCATAS
CALIENTES FRIOS
HAMBURGUESA 4.50 JAMON 5.60
COMPL 5.20 QUESO 4.50
BIKINI 4.50 CHORIZO 4.80
LOMO 5.20 JAMON YORK 4.50
CALAMARES 6.60 ATUN 4.80
FRANKFURT 4.50

centre ciutat
BARCELONA
BARCELONA
platja barceloneta

292

FONDUE SUIZA 140
OFERTA BOMBONES 100
JAMON SERRANO 185
CAFE 105

Store business cards and chocolate bars feature photos of sun-drenched scenes and tasty local delights.

Elusive Exclusives

Luxurious and avant-garde? Yes. Intimidating and ostentatious? No. These super-desirables are exclusive, not due to elitism or ridiculous prices, but because they target a design savvy, fashion-conscious crowd for whom every surface is an opportunity for visual and tactile beauty. Themed collections and catalogs revolve around concepts inspired by art and culture. Interiors are conceived by artists and architects. Invitations, tags and packaging are embossed, varnished and foil-stamped, resulting in miniature ornaments that add to the fascination. It is an environment created for the cultivated and initiated.

Preen

StudioThomson, www.studiothomson.com

Everything a cult fashion label needs to be, Preen by Justin Thornton and Thea Bregazzi is a class act that attracts stylists, media types and celebrities alike, thanks to beautiful clothes with a strong and individual look. StudioThomson's sophisticated branding wittily translates the different collection themes and influences into tangible items in the form of exquisite invites and print pieces.

5 Portobello Green
281 Portobello Road
London W10 5TZ
United Kingdom
www.preen.eu

The Fall/Winter 04-05 promotional poster features backstage photographs from the catwalk show.

PREEN BY THORNTON BREGAZZI
AUTUMN WINTER 2004|5

297

PREEN BY
THORNTON BREGAZZI
SPRING SUMMER 2005
TUESDAY 21ST
SEPTEMBER AT 2:30 PM
30 GRESHAM STREET
LONDON EC2
ST PAULS TUBE STATION
NAME
BLOCK
ROW
RSVP
E relativepr@aol.com
T 020 7704 8866
F 020 7704 8877

SPONSORED BY
TOPSHOP

GenerationPress

PREEN
BY
THORNTON BREGAZZI

An invite inspired by African prints, a logo-debossed swing tag and woven garment labels.

300

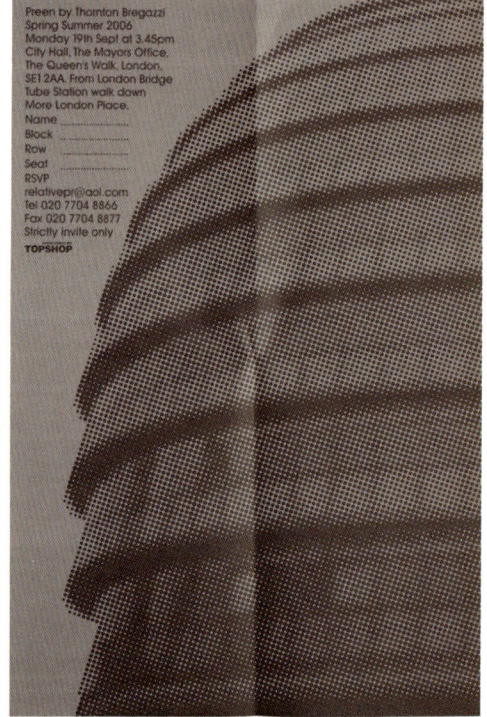

Embossed invitation (top)

PREEN BY
THORNTON BREGAZZI
SPRING SUMMER 2007
TUESDAY 19 SEPTEMBER
AT 12:30 PM
THE GREAT HALL
THE WEST STAND
STAMFORD BRIDGE
FOOTBALL STADIUM
CHELSEA VILLAGE
FULHAM ROAD SW6
RSVP
INFO@RELATIVEPR.COM
020 7704 8866

TOPSHOP

Invitation (bottom left)

Preen by Thornton Bregazzi
Spring Summer 2006
Monday 19th Sept at 3.45pm
City Hall, The Mayors Office,
The Queen's Walk, London,
SE1 2AA. From London Bridge
Tube Station walk down
More London Place.

Name _____
Block _____
Row _____
Seat _____
RSVP
relativepr@aol.com
tel 020 7704 8866
Fax 020 7704 8877
Strictly invite only

TOPSHOP

Invitation (bottom right)

PREEN
by
thornton
bregazzi
autumn
winter
2005/6

tuesday
15th
february
3.30pm

the
great
hall

the
west
stand

stamford
bridge
football
stadium

chelsea
village

fulham
road

sw6
lhs

fulham
broadway
tube

london
fashion
week
return
bus
service
available
from
front
of
bfc
tent

name
_____
block
_____
row
_____

RSVP
relativepr
@aol.com

telephone
020
7704
8866

facsimile
020
7704
8877

TOPSHOP

Invites inspired by *2001: A Space Odyssey*, polka dots, children's spelling books and geometric shapes.

PREEN
BY
THORNTON BREGAZZI

DECADE

Spreads from a hardcover book to celebrate 10 years of Preen by Thornton Bregazzi.

AFRICAN HOBBIE
Spring Summer 2005

Held in a vast metal floored glass office space, in the heart of the city of London, the collection took inspiration from the 1970's 'Holly Hobbie' character and African textiles, crafts and techniques.

Photography - Tim Bret-Day
Styling - Ursula Hugh

A t-shirt print based on invite artwork, and an invite based on a collection of textured materials.

PREEN BY
THORNTON
BREGAZZI
AUTUMN /
WINTER 2007-8
WEDNESDAY
14 FEBRUARY
AT 10.45 AM
LORDS CRICKET
GROUND
NURSERY
PAVILION
NORTH ENTRANCE
WELLINGTON RD
OFF PARK RD
NW1. RSVP
LFW@RELATIVEPR
.COM TEL 020
7704 8866   TOPSHOP

NAME_____

_____

BLOCK___ROW___

Mahna Mahna

Three & Co., www.three-co.jp

An exclusive boutique in Tokyo, Mahna Mahna supplies to professional stylists only. The shop is extensively stocked with designer wear and vintage pieces, from shoes and accessories to gowns and swimwear, which are rented out for photo shoots. Three & Co. designed the logo and print identity, with shop cards resembling clothes tags in order to be easily recognized as a fashion store.

5-12-28 Minami-Aoyama,
Minato-ku
Tokyo 107-0062
Japan
www.mahna.co.jp

Mahna Mahna also stocks men's collections, and has an online shop that is open to the public.

307

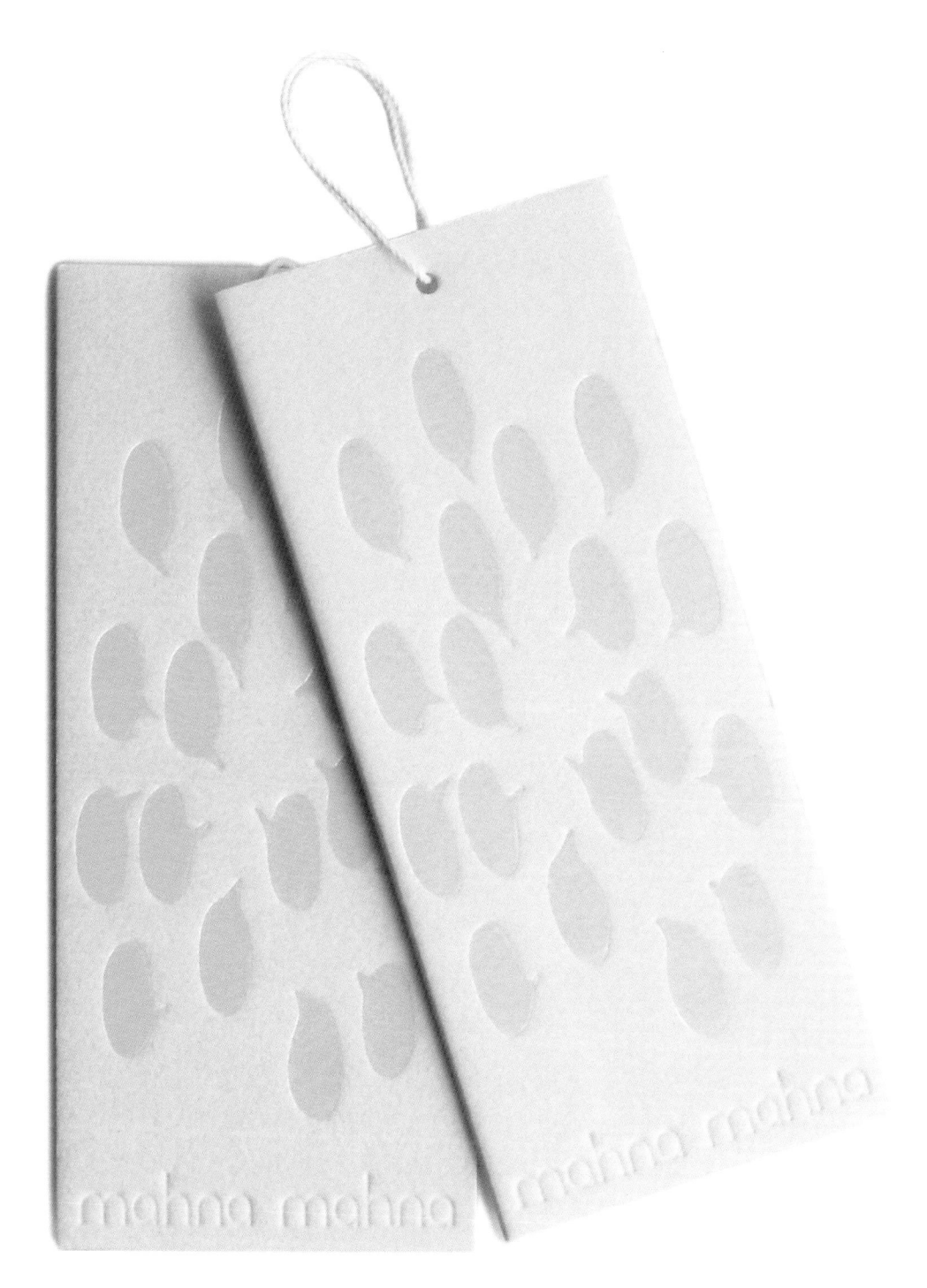

308

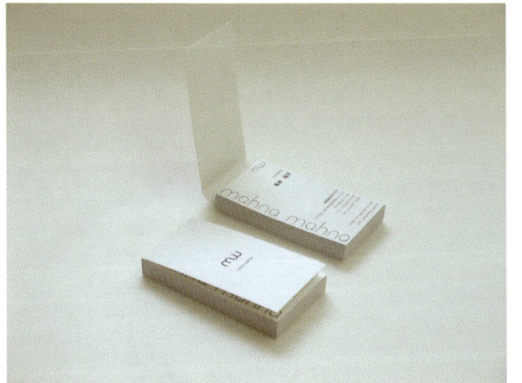

The business cards are designed to look like memo pads and ease card-exchanging.

309

Expo Nova

Mission Design, www.mission.no

A top-shelf luxury furniture retailer, Expo Nova needed a visual rebranding that reflected their quality products and exclusive furniture lines. Mission Design stepped up to the challenge and designed a retail concept based on an elegant custom typography, paying special attention to the X, beautiful photography of natural materials and brightly colored store signage.

Bygdøy allé 69
Pb 554 Skøyen
0214 Oslo
Norway
www.expo-nova.no

The new Expo Nova store is organized in sections imitating a city apartment.

311

EXPO NOVA
+
B&B ITALIA

Expo Nova Møbel
Bygdøy allé 69
Telefon 2313140

Expo Nova Kontrakt
Bygdøy allé 68
Telefon 2313140

Expo Nova Lys
Bygdøy allé 59
Telefon 2313140

www.expo-nova.no

EXPO NOVA

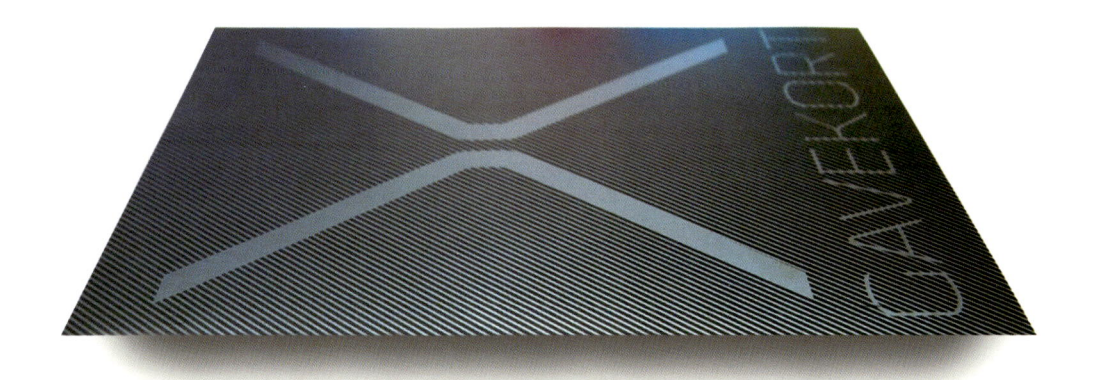

The simple and refined graphic profile emphasizes Expo Nova as a supplier of design classics.

EXPO NOVA

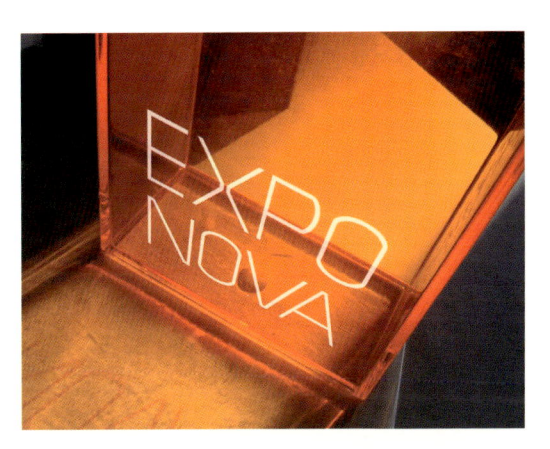

Natural textures on labels and carrier bags contrast with the bright colors of the indoor signage.

Hayashi

HORT, www.hort.org.uk

Multi-disciplinary studio and creative hub HORT were commissioned by luxury boutique Hayashi to come up with a visual system that would match its stance – progressive and avant-garde. Irregular handmade art juxtaposed on simple, clean-cut carrier bags and cards provided the basics for unconventionally attractive images, further refined by the addition of wall graphics and promotional materials.

Börsenplatz 13-15
60313 Frankfurt
Germany
www.hayashi-shop.com

Fashion and art mingle in the 130 m² space, packed with eclectic clothes, shoes and accessories.

317

318

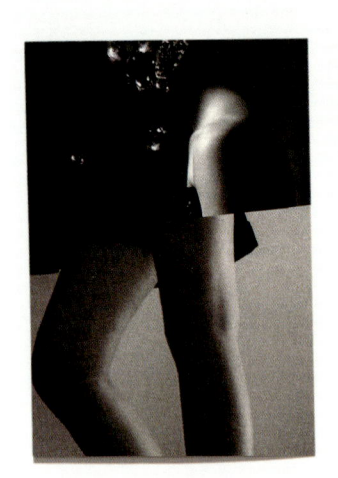

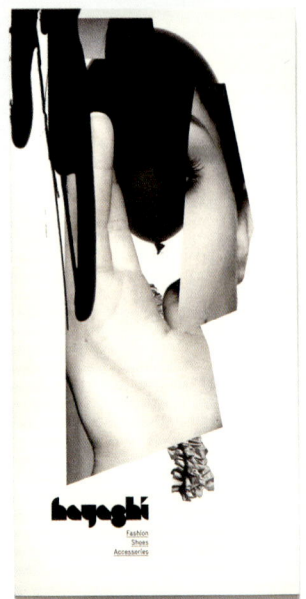

The corporate identity keeps the ad-hoc feel with art collages made from fashion images.

319

320

Larger-scale collages on the walls set the mood and help to highlight the clothes.

Melynas

It is Blank, www.itisblank.com

A Lithuanian multi-disciplinary studio based in Vilnus, It is Blank works as a network of independent artists. When designing the visual identity for Melynas, a multi-brand designer boutique, it was decided that since the various labels sold in the shop were so different from each other, the shop's identity should be subtle. The designed material uses a simple black-and-white color scheme.

Jogailos g. 6
Vilnius, 01116
Lithuania
www.naujoji-europa.lt

The logo and signage instantly became a well-known icon in Vilnius, equivalent with emerging fashion.

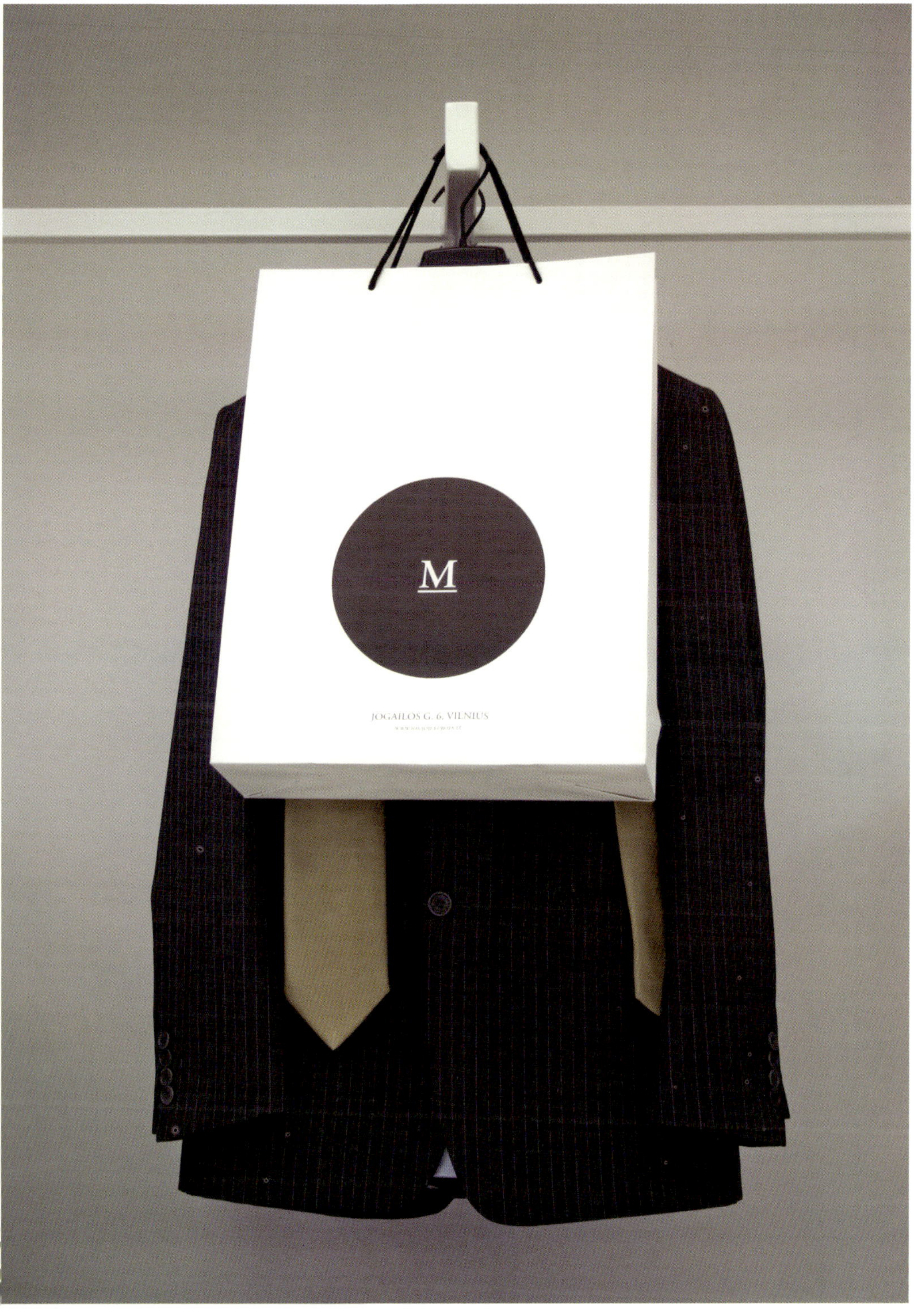
M
JOGAILOS G. 6, VILNIUS

The strong and simple identity successfully unites the various brands sold in the shop.

325

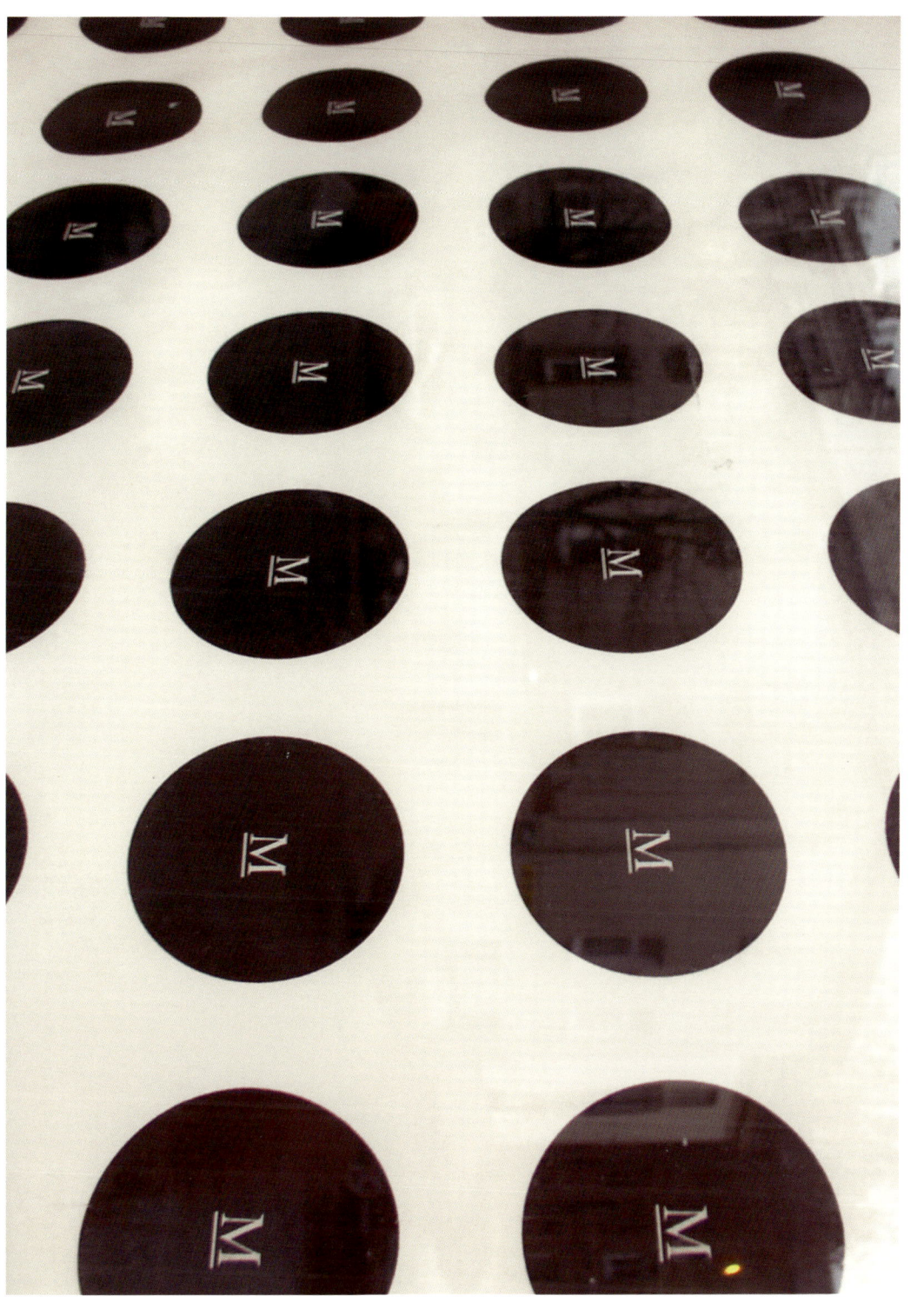

Pedro García

Cla-se, www.cla-se.com

Originally a small family business making children's shoes, today Pedro García is an internationally exported luxury women's footwear brand. Known for their refined branding schemes, Cla-se studio was commissioned to come up with a global corporal identity program for the label — a full line of packaging, communication material, supervision of store interiors and web design.

Calle de Jorge Juan, 14, local 3
28001 Madrid
Spain
www.pedrogarcia.com

Pedro García footwear is aimed at women who are aware of trends and look for quality products.

pedro garcía

pedro garcía
pol. campo alto, c/italia 46
03600 elda, alicante/españa
tel +34 96 539 90 07
fax +34 96 539 48 46
info@pedrogarcia.com
www.pedrogarcia.com

pedro garcía
pol. campo alto, c/italia 46
03600 elda, alicante/españa
tel +34 96 539 90 07
fax +34 96 539 48 46
info@pedrogarcia.com
www.pedrogarcia.com
pedro garcía/store
c/ jorge juan, 14
callejón, local 3
28001 madrid/españa
tel/fax +34 91 575 34 41
info@pedrogarcia.com
www.pedrogarcia.com

Less is more – a range of simple shoeboxes and kraft paper bags keep the packaging sleek and simple.

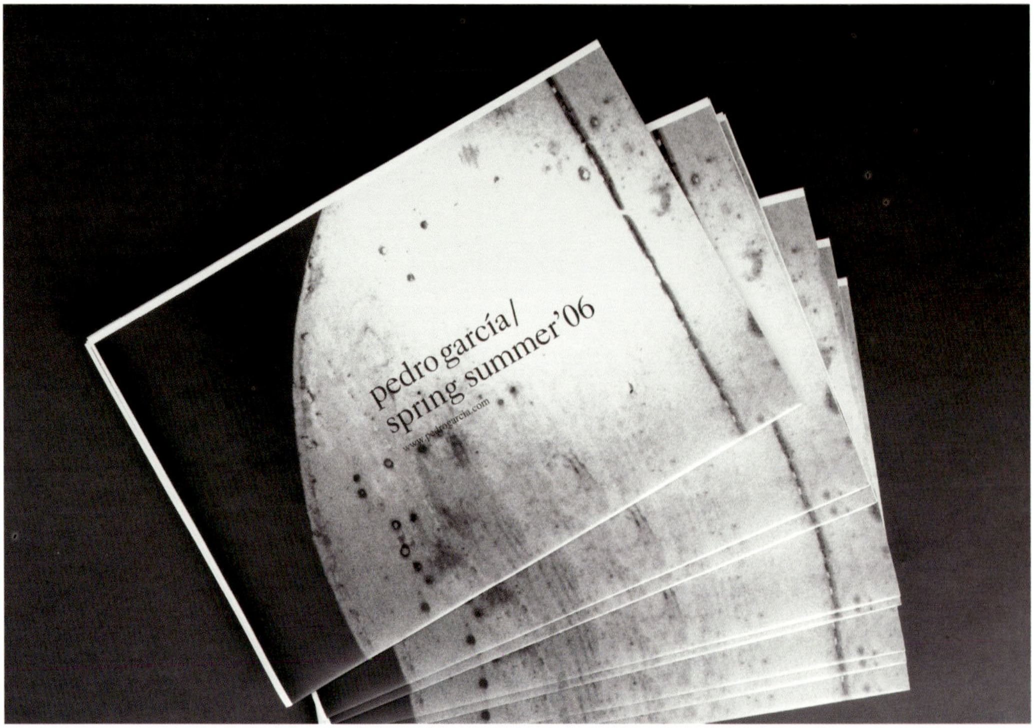
pedro garcía/
spring summer'06
www.pedrogarcia.com

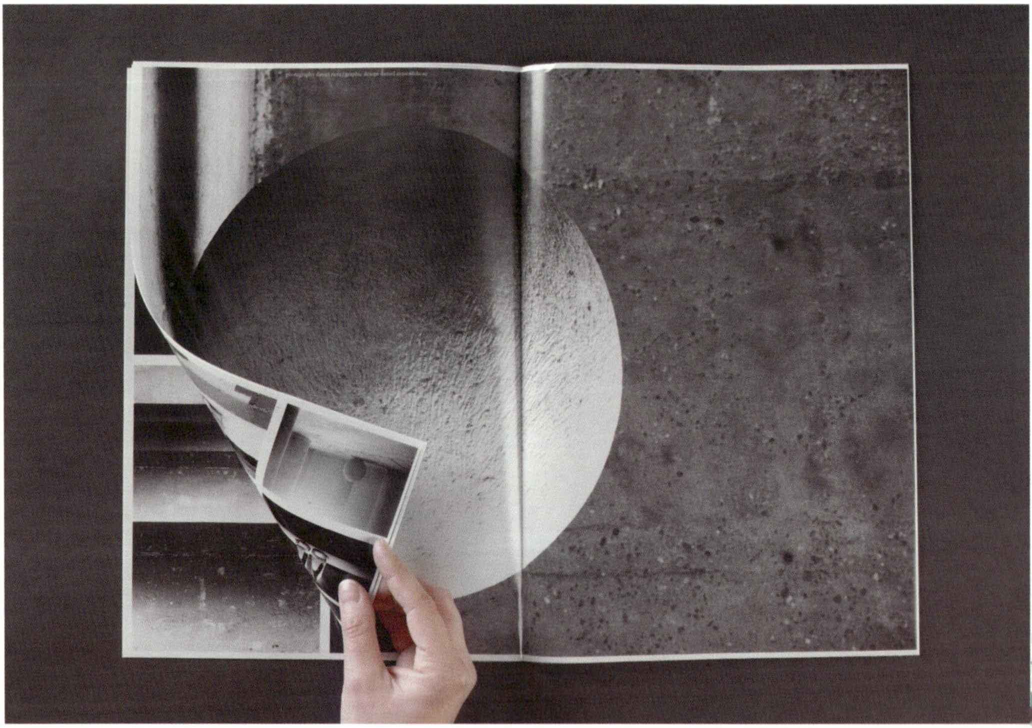

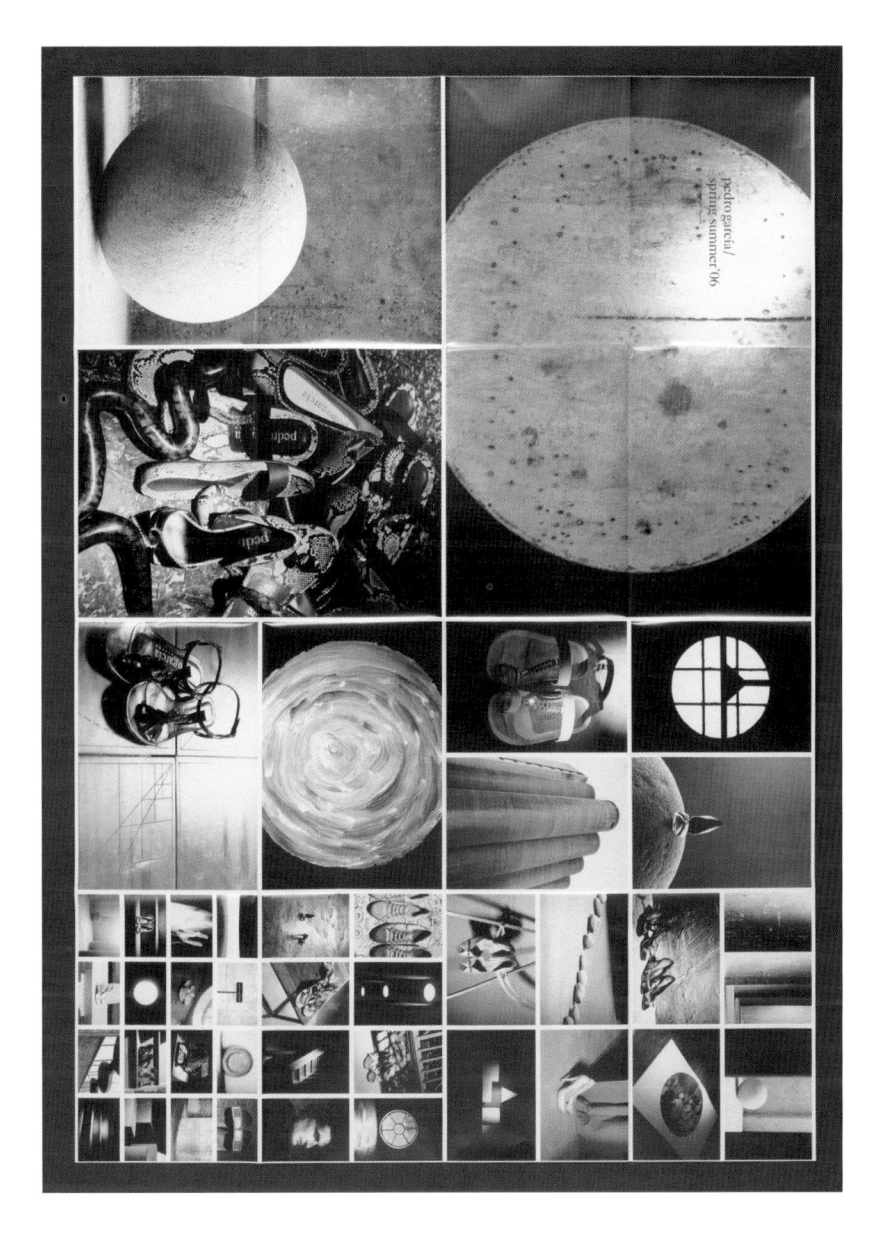

The Spring/Summer 06 black-and-white catalog is reminiscent of surrealist photography.

332

UNITED SALVAGE CO.
The
pedrogarcía
autumn winter
&
05.06
collection

The catalog for Fall/Winter 06 folds out into a jumbo-sized poster covered in a cluster of creative stills.

334

The catalogs for 2005 included postcards and posters featuring intimate interior product shots.